SKELETON COAST

SKELETON COAST

Amy Schoeman

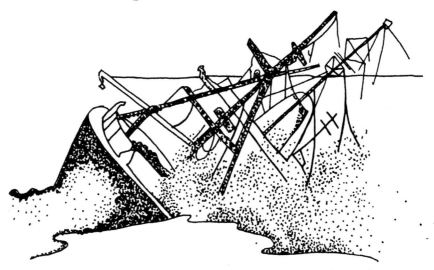

Illustrations by Janet Lautenbach

SOUTHERN
BOOK PUBLISHERS

Previously published by
Macmillan South Africa (Publishers) (Pty) Ltd

ISBN 1 86812 081 3

First edition, first impression 1988
Published by
Southern Book Publishers (Pty) Ltd
PO Box 548, Bergvlei 2012
Johannesburg

Illustrations by Janet Lautenbach
Set in 11 on 13 pt Garamond
by Unifoto, Cape Town
Printed and bound by
CTP Book Printers, Cape

BD8542

CONTENTS

This book is dedicated to the memory of my son,
KENDALL ALUN COSBURN
who was killed in a motor car accident, at the age of
fifteen, while I was working on the text

Preface

M Y FIRST VISIT to the Skeleton Coast was in October 1977. I went as photo/journalist for the then Division of Nature Conservation and Tourism to obtain material for an article on the area. I found it visually so captivating that I subsequently returned on many occasions to take photographs, the culmination of which is the selection presented in this book.

It was on this first trip that I met my husband, Louw Schoeman, whose enthusiasm for the area was infectious and who, from the outset, aroused my interest in its long-term conservation. By this time he had already been closely associated with the Skeleton Coast for more than twenty years. Practising as a lawyer in Windhoek, he initially came to know the area through clients interested in prospecting, and subsequently became involved in the search for diamonds himself. As a director of the original Westies Minerals Company, he played a leading role in the formation of the consortium which planned the building of a harbour and the development of an infrastructure. As founder and director of the Sarusas Development Corporation, he actively participated in the research and other activities undertaken by the company. When the South African Government unilaterally withdrew from the scheme, his appreciation of the area caused him to direct his attention to its conservation.

He persuaded his group to donate the research station, workshop and vehicles at Möwe Bay, as well as an amount of money, to the Division of Nature Conservation and Tourism for the establishment of the first nature conservation control post at the Skeleton Coast. This added momentum to efforts to have the area proclaimed as a park, as was originally envisaged in the Odendaal Plan. By establishing a fly-in safari service from Windhoek to the Skeleton Coast, he has since pioneered the development of a limited and controlled form of tourism in the wilderness section of the park.

He believes that in the long run an area can be protected as a wilderness reserve only if the public is given the opportunity to visit it. In this way appreciation and understanding of its value are stimulated and the idea of protecting it can be promoted. Equally at home behind the controls of an aircraft or the steering-wheel of a Landrover, he has spent many thousands of hours flying, driving and walking over this remote terrain, and today knows it better than most.

The conservation aspect of the area has become increasingly prevalent: the sensitivity of the desert surface to vehicle tracks; the mounds, trenches and rusting machinery left by miners and prospectors; the dwindling numbers of game; and, most of all, the necessity and desirability to conserve it as a wilderness reserve to which access is limited and development is kept to a minimum. Other than the visual beauty of the terrain, these aspects are also depicted in the photographs and have been the underlying motive for writing the book.

Vehicle tracks are a major form of pollution in the desert and one of Louw Schoeman's constant headaches. They disfigure what would otherwise be an unspoilt landscape and, especially on the gravel plains, could take hundreds of years to disappear.

ACKNOWLEDGEMENTS

My husband, Louw, assisted me immeasurably with his broad general knowledge of the Skeleton Coast, both in the preparation of the text and, as pilot, driver and guide, in obtaining the photographic material for this book. For this, as well as his unfailing encouragement, enthusiasm and patience throughout the project, I would like to thank him especially.

I am grateful to Mike Müller, Curator of the State Herbarium, Windhoek, Dr Roy Miller, Director of Geological Survey, Windhoek, and Riaan van Zyl of the Weather Bureau, J. G. Strijdom Airport, who assisted with the preparation of the sections on plants, geology and climate respectively, by prior discussion and subsequent revision of the initial drafts. Mrs Estelle van Hoepen of the Botanical Research Institute, Pretoria, checked the plant names in the final draft, for which I should also like to express my appreciation.

Thank you to Mike and Eryn Griffin who assisted with the section on fauna, and to Götz Wohlers of Swakopmund, Ernst Karlowa of Swakopmund and Hein Altmann of Walvis Bay who supplied sources and information on the history of the area.

I would also like to thank my colleague Janet Lautenbach, both for accomplishing the illustrations and map and for her useful advice during the final revision of the text.

PROLOGUE

'Wednesday, 26 September 1900. We saddle the horses before daybreak. It is very cold and the wind is still blowing. Further southwards along the beach we experience the same problem as yesterday with the two unwilling horses. In addition the wind is getting worse. As the wind turns more southerly it develops by 7 o'clock into a sandstorm. It is ice cold, we are virtually frozen. The air is filled with sand. One can see barely five yards ahead. The sun hangs like a dull disc in the sky. Apart from the sand the storm also brings small stones the size of peas, which with their sharp teeth scratch and lash against our faces. With eyes tightly closed we forge our way ahead. We can only ride at a snail's pace against the storm. My hope that we might still reach Angra Fria today is rapidly fading. The situation is becoming critical.

By 8 o'clock we are making virtually no progress. The horses refuse to walk against the storm. We are forced to dismount on an open plain near the beach. There is not a single sand-dune behind which we can shelter, we are surrounded by a sea of sand. We place the saddles upright with the saddle blankets behind and lie flat on the ground, sheltering, with our heads behind the saddles. Although not much, this does help a little. Everything fills up with sand; eyes, ears, nose and mouth, all pockets and openings. The situation is becoming increasingly serious. Josiah is hopeful that by noon the storm will have subsided. We lie patiently still until noon. We are virtually covered in sand. The storm rages on.

Rightly or wrongly, I decide to saddle the horses and proceed. With great difficulty we manage to get the saddle blankets and saddles on the horses. The storm is blowing so forcefully that we can hardly stand. At a slow walk we proceed along the beach against the storm. Very soon one of the horses, Peter, gives in. Despite beating him, he refuses to move and we are forced to leave him behind. All we can now do is: 'Forward!' Very soon the second horse, Jonker, collapses. We are obliged to leave the pack saddle as well as the horse behind. The situation is now becoming extremely serious. If the other two horses also give in, we are lost. I realise that proceeding further south against the storm is no longer a proposition. All that remains is a choice between making our way back to the Kunene or riding at right angles to the storm and forging our way directly eastwards. According to my estimation we are between 45-50 kilometres away from the Kunene, that is, halfway between the Kunene and Angra Fria. I make a quick decision: we will ride towards the east. I do this both to get the hungry horses to grazing as soon as possible and to humour Josiah, who has continually requested me to turn back to the Kunene. In the meanwhile the storm rages on.

After an hour we have left the coastal plains behind us. We are ascending a range of rocky and stony hillocks. At 4 o'clock in the afternoon we unsaddle for an hour. Then on again, up and down without a break, but gradually climbing higher. We find ourselves on the western escarpment of the Namib Plateau which is bounded towards the sea by rows of hills. By riding at right angles to the storm the going is slightly easier. Carefully and slowly we proceed. At the steep places we dismount and lead the horses so as not to overstrain them. Thus we travel for half the night. The storm blows at its worst on the rises, it goes through bone and marrow. Josiah's entire body is shivering from the cold. By midnight the storm is again blowing so forcefully that we have to off-saddle behind a granite boulder in which there is a slight hollow. We crawl into the hollow, heads first, but our bodies are exposed to the storm outside and are soon covered by sand. We hold the horses by their bridles. Like this we await the morning.

Before daybreak we saddle the horses. I am worried about Josiah. His entire body is shaking from the cold, and no less my own. To our joy the storm gradually starts to subside. We proceed further in an easterly direction. It is discouraging that we see no end to the rows and rows of hillocks that we are crisscrossing. Hardly have we climbed one ridge than the next one, which we had not seen while travelling between the ridges, rises up in front of us. By 7 o'clock the third horse also collapses. If the fourth horse fails to hold out we are lost. I don't think that I will be able to travel the rest of the way to Nadas on foot as we are already extremely tired. Josiah offers voluntarily to walk, although he is already carrying a blanket, his gun, his bandolier and a water-bag which is half full. The remaining horse, the balky, dapple-grey Hans, is still going very well. I have a more than half full water-bag with which I can easily last another day. In provisions we still have a hand-sized piece of springbok meat. We proceed slowly and carefully, clambering over one rise after the other.

Finally, we reach the highest point at 9 o'clock and see, stretched out ahead of us, the mighty Namib plain and far to the east the peak of Omatjenguma. Now at last we can see an objective, an end ahead of us. My calculations at least were correct: I had estimated that we would come out more or less facing Omatjenguma. We rest awhile and then descend into the valley ahead of us, which is filled with heavy sand-dunes. In the meantime the wind has died down and the heat of the sun is becoming very oppressive. Tired beyond measure, we scramble over the sand-dunes and in the afternoon reach a dry river-bed where we encounter the first tree, a small stunted specimen, in the shadow of which we dismount. In the sand-dunes a herd of gemsbok thunders past without our being able to take a shot. Our rifles are so full of sand that we are unable to open and load them. Under this most welcome dwarf tree we devour the last morsel of springbok meat. Then we fall immediately into a deep sleep. Our Hans also puts his head under the shade of the tree and sleeps. He is too thirsty to graze, although there is grazing available. Thus we remain until about 3 o'clock when we proceed to clean our rifles as best we can before moving on at 4 o'clock.'

Translated extract from the diary of Dr Georg Hartmann, on an attempted survey of the coastline between the Kunene River and Angra Fria.

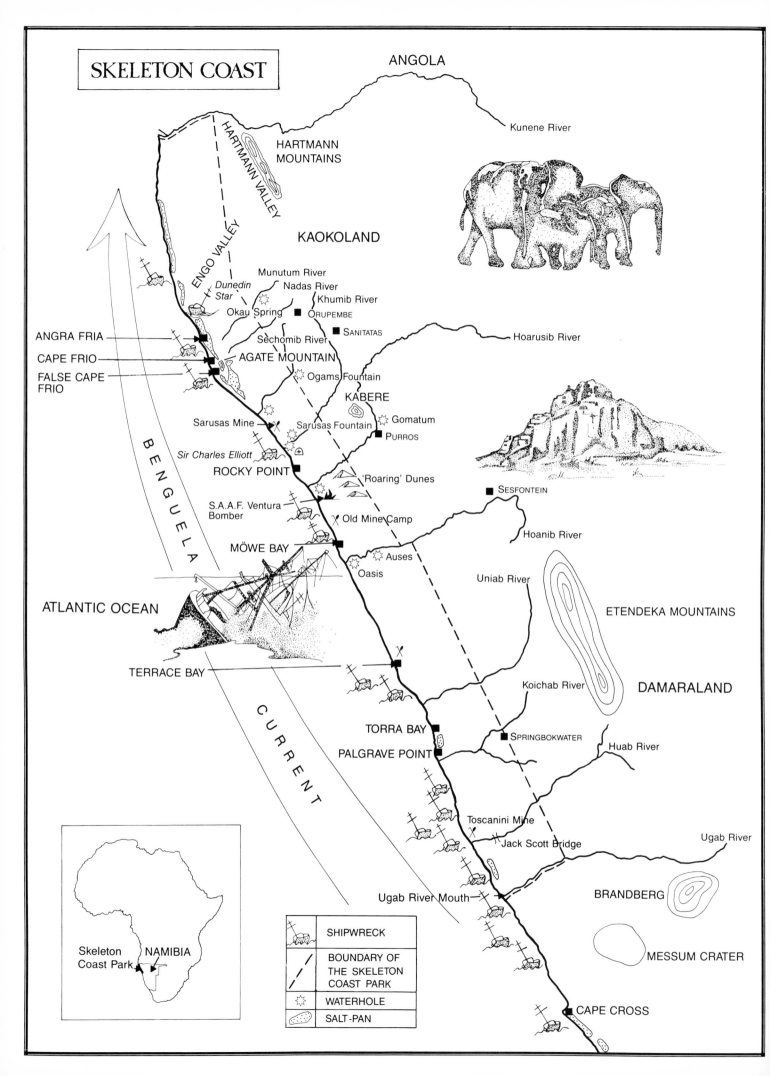

SKELETON COAST

ANGOLA

Kunene River

HARTMANN MOUNTAINS

HARTMANN VALLEY

ENGO VALLEY

KAOKOLAND

Dunedin Star

Munutum River
Nadas River
Khumib River

Okau Spring
ORUPEMBE

SANITATAS

Hoarusib River

ANGRA FRIA
CAPE FRIO
FALSE CAPE FRIO

AGATE MOUNTAIN

Sechomib River

Ogams Fountain

KABERE

Sarusas Mine
Sarusas Fountain

Gomatum

Sir Charles Elliott

PURROS

ROCKY POINT

'Roaring' Dunes

SESFONTEIN

S.A.A.F. Ventura Bomber

Old Mine Camp

Hoanib River

MÖWE BAY

Auses

Oasis

Uniab River

ATLANTIC OCEAN

ETENDEKA MOUNTAINS

BENGUELA

TERRACE BAY

Koichab River

DAMARALAND

CURRENT

TORRA BAY
PALGRAVE POINT

SPRINGBOKWATER

Huab River

Toscanini Mine
Jack Scott Bridge

Ugab River

Ugab River Mouth

BRANDBERG

Skeleton Coast Park   NAMIBIA

MESSUM CRATER

⚓	SHIPWRECK
/	BOUNDARY OF THE SKELETON COAST PARK
✦	WATERHOLE
⬭	SALT-PAN

CAPE CROSS

INTRODUCTION

The portion of the South West African/Namibian coastline popularly referred to as the Skeleton Coast extends from the Kunene River in the north to Cape Cross in the south. It is part of the Namib Desert and has as its hinterland the western sections of Kaokoland and Damaraland. In former years the area was referred to as the Kaokoveld coast, before the countless skeletons of ships and men along its shores gave rise to the evocative name 'Skeleton Coast'.

The creation of the Skeleton Coast Park dates back to 1963 when, mainly for political reasons, the narrow tract of coastline approximately 30 to 40 kilometres wide and 500 kilometres long, situated between the Ugab and the Kunene Rivers, was set aside as a future nature reserve. Since the inception of the park in 1971 it has been managed by the Directorate of Nature Conservation as a wilderness area, that is, an area where development is kept to a minimum and to which the public has limited access.

Within its present boundaries, however, the park is not a closed ecological unit. The courses of rivers such as the Hoarusib, Khumib, Hoanib, Uniab and Ugab are essential ingredients of the ecological circuit, but lie to a large extent outside the park's boundaries. These linear oases with their riverine vegetation and series of waterholes are the subsistence of the springbok, gemsbok, ostrich, jackal, leopard, brown hyaena and baboon of the park. They are also the stamping grounds of endangered species such as the desert-adapted elephant, black rhino, giraffe and lion, which roam up and down the dry river-beds in search of food and water. When the animals go beyond the confines of the park into the adjacent Kaoko- and Damaraland they are at the mercy of poachers and trophy hunters, and as a result their numbers have decreased in recent years at an alarming rate. To constitute a self-contained ecological unit and ensure the protection of the wildlife in the area, the eastern border of the park should be extended further eastwards, at least as far as the 100-mm-rainfall line. Ideally, a link-up corridor between the Skeleton Coast Park and the Etosha National Park should be created to allow for animal migration.

Not only the wildlife but also the landscape is threatened by people who gain access to the park, both lawfully and unlawfully. Far too often they leave an appalling array of tracks, trenches and tin-cans in their wake, the after-effects of which are both extensive and lasting. Few people realise how sensitive the surface of the desert is to vehicle tracks, especially the harder surfaces of the gravel plains. Tyres break the hard top layer and leave tracks which, in human terms, could be permanent. According to experts, tracks on the harder surfaces could take anything from 700 to 1000 years to disappear. As the result of prospecting there are areas in the park that are crisscrossed and scarred by myriads of tracks, at places resembling multi-laned highways leading in all directions. In addition to being unsightly, the tracks do untold damage to the lichen fields of the gravel plains.

Where prospecting has led to mining the defacement has been even more extensive. Rusting machinery, disintegrating oil rigs, corroding drills and heaps of indescribable rubbish have given the abandoned mining sites an ambience of waste, neglect and abject desolation. On a smaller scale are the innumerable and sad little heaps of sifted sand, silent testimonies of the magnetic attraction that the desert has for optimistic prospectors and fortune hunters.

The graphic quality of sand patterns and textures presents endless possibilities for the photographer.

This magnetism has other facets. For the photographer, the attraction of the Skeleton Coast lies essentially in its landscape and it is this aspect which is primarily portrayed by the photographs in this book. The wide horizons, the variety of colour, texture and form and the ever-changing moods of light and shadow are a feast through the lens of a camera, albeit often a very elusive one. Light conditions are unpredictable and change so rapidly that a scene which one minute has profile, dimension and contrast is flat and colourless the next.

The text is primarily concerned with those aspects of the area which are of human interest; with the fates of those who did not go there voluntarily but were forcibly cast up on its inhospitable shores by the vagaries of the elements, in many cases to die a lonely and agonising death; with the courage and enterprise of the early explorers and pioneers who attempted to open it up to civilisation but, because of its nature, largely failed; and with the interest value of its desert-adapted flora and fauna and the many other aspects which make it one of the most unusual desert environments in the world. Today its very isolation has become its attraction, an isolation that made Aristotle Onassis exclaim, as he looked around at the wide expanse of endless desert landscape on a visit to the Skeleton Coast in 1966: 'What magnificent solitude!'

An interesting aspect which emerges is that modern technology has gradually changed people's attitude to the Skeleton Coast. Where it was initially a place to fear and avoid, it has now become a place which is sought after for its beauty, silence and solitude. There is an irony in the thought that the very technology which brought this about, at the same time threatens to destroy its attraction.

Weird and fantastically shaped rocks stimulate the imagination, resembling anything from Charles de Gaulle's nose to a polar bear.

15

The Geology

... forces that shaped the desert profile

THE DESERT IMPARTS a pervasive sense of timelessness as perspective takes on new dimensions, horizons expand into infinity and space is amplified around, above and beyond. One instinctively feels that the landscape as it is today cannot be much different from what it was a thousand, ten thousand or even ten million years ago. Glass-like pieces of lava, which boiled, bubbled, burst and solidified aeons ago, are so well preserved that they might have been created in a cataclysm that occurred yesterday. To a geologist, the landscape must read like an open book, its components exposed and uncluttered by vegetation and rural or urban development.

The oldest types of rock found at the Skeleton Coast today are mica schist, gneiss and granite. They are part of the Damara sequence which was deposited between 1 000 and 700 million years ago and became buried deep within the crust of the earth about 600 to 700 million years ago. Today the granites — molten rock which crystallised deep within the bowels of the earth — are clearly visible at Möwe Bay as a striking mosaic of grey granite, cut by grey dolerite dykes and pink feldspar gravels. Behind the dune belt, between the Khumib and the Hoarusib Rivers, large flat, blue-grey tables of gneiss emerge, sometimes veined with white quartz or studded with pink feldspar, lying more or less level with the surface. Just south of the Hoanib River low ridges of a reddish-brown gneiss

1 A panoramic vista of the red-brick and brown igneous rock formations of the Etendeka lavas of Damaraland, hinterland of the Skeleton Coast. Whitish-grey lichen, which is sustained by moisture blown inland from the sea, clings to the south-western mountain slopes.

appear and, running parallel to the coast, cut across the Hoanib and Khumib Rivers past Ogams Fountain and through to the Hartmann Valley. The reddish and grey minerals within the gneiss are different types of feldspar, set in a fine-grained groundmass of quartz and mica.

Towards the coast outcrops of these granitic and gneissic rocks become pitted and eroded by chemical weathering, caused possibly by salts contained in the coastal fog that penetrates inland during the night. This results in the unusual honeycomb-like patterning, which makes the rocks so striking and picturesque. Some take on the appearance of giant molten toadstools, others have hollow, ghost-like features and have therefore been aptly named the 'petrified ghosts' of the Skeleton Coast.

The most impressive of the mica schists are seen in the Ugab River Valley, surrounding the Brandberg West mine, west of the Brandberg. The mica schists were initially deep sea muds, which became folded and concertinaed by enormous horizontal pressures and now occur as numerous north-south ridges. They are blue, grey, yellow and brown in colour, and sometimes contain bands of grey and brown marble. As the ancient mountain ranges of granite, gneiss and mica schist become increasingly eroded, a low-lying stretch of land between the coast and the escarpment was formed, a geographical feature which became known as the 'Namib platform'.

At the beginning of the Karoo period, some 350 million years ago, the interior of what is today Southern Africa was covered by a vast sheet of ice. Large westward-moving glaciers deposited glacial debris, boulders, gravel and sand on the Namib platform and at the same time gouged out several deep valleys, into which the Kunene, Engo, Munutum, Nadas, Khumib and Gomadommi Rivers were destined to drain. As the climate changed, the ice gradually melted and the landmass warmed up, these deposits were transported westwards by river flood-waters and can today still be seen in the vicinity of the Kunene and Hoanib Rivers.

About 200 million years ago, during the early Jurassic period, the first layer of windblown sand was deposited. These early dunes hardened to form a conspicuous yellowish-brown sandstone which can be seen in the Huab Valley and around Cape Frio.

CONTINENTAL DRIFT

In younger Mesozoic times, about 120 to 170 million years ago, the supercontinent of the southern hemisphere, known as Gondwanaland, began to break apart as the African and South American continents slowly drifted away from each other, a process which is still in progress today. During this rifting deep fissures opened in the crust of the earth and vast quantities of lava were squeezed out of its bowels, to spread like a large flat cake over the Namib platform. These flood lavas or Karoo basalts are called the Etendeka lavas and, when one is flying along the coast, can be seen clearly from the air. They start at the Erongo Mountains in the interior and on the Skeleton Coast just north of Cape Cross, surrounding the Messum Crater and covering a huge area north of the Huab River. This extends to Grootberg in the east, while sporadic outcrops range from the Uniab River mouth to Orupembe and the Hartmann Mountains. These lavas appear along the coast at Terrace Bay and again just north of Möwe Bay through Rocky Point up to Cape Frio, and run parallel to the coastline as low-lying ridges. Further inland they form towering flat-topped mountains.

The mica schists surrounding the old Brandberg West Mine became folded and concertinaed by enormous horizontal pressures, millions of years ago, and now occur as numerous north-south ridges.

Overleaf

2　With Angola on its northern and Namibia on its southern banks the Kunene River, northern boundary of the Skeleton Coast, forges its way through awesome mountain ranges to the Atlantic Ocean.

3　Smoothly sculptured dune ridges 'smoke' as they are shaped and reshaped by the prevailing winds. For the greater part of the year the prevailing wind is south or south-west and the slipfaces face north. In winter when the east winds blow the ridges change their attitude and assume a knife-edge appearance.

4　Despite its straggly and unassuming appearance, the brack-bush or coastal ganna, **Salsola nollothensis**, is highly nutritious and favoured especially by springbok. It generally grows in association with a dune and obtains its moisture from dew and coastal fog.

Mostly basaltic in composition, the Etendeka lavas are unique in chemistry among Southern African lavas, but are identical to the Parana lavas of Brazil, a huge lava field which covers an area about ten times the size of the Etendeka lavas. This is one of the many geological features that supports the theory of continental drift.

The brick-red, brown, grey and black lavas contain amethyst, agate, carnelian, jasper and moss agate which formed in bubble-like gas cavities trapped in the cooling rock. Fluids seeped into these cavities and deposited silica in finely crystalline forms such as amethyst. The latter can be quite spectacular and is found in large hollow geodes which consist of several growth layers. The centre layer of amethyst crystals varies from a light mauve to a dark opulent purple, and has crystallised onto a wider layer of white quartz crystals, which is surrounded by a dense layer of agate and then a rough outer crust of chalcedony. There was a time when amethyst geodes could be found lying loose on the surface, but these have all long since been removed. Normally, they are mined by blasting them with dynamite out of the solid rock in which they are embedded. The geodes sometimes crack open with the blasting, but generally have to be forcibly broken open with hammers. These enormous solidified gas bubbles range from approximately 15 cm in diameter to about 50 cm or more. Amethyst geodes which are large enough for a man to crouch in have been found on the Skeleton Coast.

2

3

4

The three largest concentrations of amethyst found on the Skeleton Coast are behind the dunes at Terrace Bay, inland from Rocky Point and at Sarusas, although they are also known to occur in other places. Amethysts have been mined at Sarusas on and off since 1965, but never in profitable quantities, partly because of the high cost of mining them in such a remote area, and partly because of the limited demand.

Agates are rather different in appearance and composition. They are smaller, not hollow inside, and of a very fine crystalline, layered chalcedony which comes in many shades of blue, grey, white, orange and yellow. The layers alternate in one or two different colours and occur in different patterns. Although agates are not particularly valuable, they lend themselves to cutting and polishing and make interesting jewellery and ornaments. They are found in large quantities on the surface at different localities on the Skeleton Coast and are much more plentiful than amethysts. A very attractive form of agate is the translucent orange or yellow cornelian which is also found in large quantities on the surface.

BRANDBERG, MESSUM AND DOROS

Lying in the hinterland of the Skeleton Coast is the awe-inspiring mountain massif, the Brandberg, at 2 574 m the highest mountain in Namibia, and clearly visible from the coast. One hundred and twenty million years ago the area was a volcano set in a vast plateau of volcanic rocks. Volcanic action on the surface was accompanied by the intrusion deep down below the volcano of a gigantic mass of granite. Subsequent erosion of the surrounding lavas gradually exposed the massive chunk of weather-resistant granite which today is known as the Brandberg. Remnants of the original lava plateau can still be seen as a collar partially surrounding the granite mountain and as huge scattered blocks. Weathering of the granite into huge boulders and overhangs provided the numerous shelters which were subsequently used by Bushmen.

The Messum Crater lies north-east of Cape Cross, between the Brandberg and the coast. It has the shape of two overlapping concentric circles and a diameter of 22 km. The sharply defined circular chains of mountains and hills and the bare light surface of sand and detritus contrasted with polished black rocks

A typical example of granitic rock which has become pitted and eroded by preferential chemical weathering.

bring to mind a stark lunar landscape. Like the Brandberg and also Cape Cross, Messum is the eroded root of an old volcano, but it has a more complex ring structure than the single plug of the Brandberg. Further north of Messum, almost in line with Torra Bay and the Brandberg, lies the Doros Crater, where interesting fossil remains and traces of copper have been found. The wide and shallow saucer-shaped extrusion appears to be superimposed on its surroundings of yellow, grey and brownish schist and granite, and has an air of not quite belonging. Doros is subvolcanic, that is, it is not a true crater, as the magma probably never reached the surface.

THE AGE OF THE NAMIB

Much has been written, said and speculated on the age of the Namib Desert. Dr Charles Koch, former entomologist of the Transvaal Museum, and later founder and Director of the Desert Ecological Research Unit at Gobabeb in the central Namib, was the first to give credence to the idea that the Namib might be extremely old. The richness and endemism of the Namib fauna, notably the tenebrionid beetles, indicated a long and undisturbed existence of such specialised forms. The result was that the Namib became popularly referred to as 'the oldest desert in the world'.

Contrary to the established idea that desertification was caused entirely by the effects of the cold Benguela Current, evidence now suggests that for the past 80 million years the area which today is the Namib Desert experienced semi-arid to arid conditions long before the full establishment of the Benguela Current system.

The potential maximum age of the Namib as a desert in the true sense of the word dates back to the formation of the bedrock bevel between the south Atlantic Ocean and the escarpment, 80 to 100 km inland. The oldest fossil dunes which occur on this bevel date back to about 65 million years and were deposited by a wind regime with very much the same wind directions as the present-day systems. Aided by oceanic density gradients, winds gradually directed the cold Benguela Current from the Antarctic up along the west coast of Southern Africa, until it reached its full development about 6 million years ago. The climatic conditions caused by the presence of the Benguela Current and its associated upwelling and cooling system have prevailed since then and maintain the Namib in its present desert form. (See also the chapter on Climate.)

MINERALS OF THE SKELETON COAST

Possibly even stronger than the feelings of dread and foreboding which the Skeleton Coast has evoked in the hearts of seafarers since time immemorial, are the fast-held convictions that, hidden under its rocks and sands, lie untold quantities of mineral wealth, treasurehouses which are there for the taking. Stories of jam jars, filled with diamonds as large as peas and buried in desperation before succumbing to hunger and thirst, have lured many an opportunist to the area, invariably to return with less than he went. The legend has persisted, and still does to this day, regardless of the fact that prospecting which has been carried out over many years by private individuals as well as by the large mining companies has proved disappointing and to date only small deposits have been located.

23

The Diamond Terraces

Diamonds do, however, occur sporadically in limited quantities at several locations along the Skeleton Coast. The best known of these are the terraces at Toscanini just north of the Huab River mouth, at Terrace Bay, just north of the Uniab River mouth, and at Möwe Bay, just north of the Hoanib River mouth. The diamonds that occur here are all alluvial, that is, they are found in marine terraces which were formed by the sea between about 8 and 20 million years ago. These diamonds originated far inland in diamond pipes and fissures which were gradually eroded and washed down to the sea. Together with other gravels and boulders, the diamonds were deposited in marine terraces which normally lie parallel to the coastline. As a result of uplift along the coast most of these marine terraces are now situated up to 35 m above sea level. Subsequent erosion has resulted in diamonds being found between the old marine terraces and the present-day beaches. Even on the beaches themselves diamonds are also occasionally picked up.

Although a few largish stones have been found, the Skeleton Coast diamonds are on average very small, approximately 6 to 8 stones to the carat. The quality of these diamonds is good, however: up to 80 per cent or more can be termed gem quality, while the rest can be used for industrial purposes. Although nowadays small gemstones are in demand by jewellers, as large stones have become too expensive, mining them at the Skeleton Coast is not an economic proposition. They occur in small pockets only, and reserves are simply not substantial enough to justify the expense.

Other Minerals

Although garnets come from different sources, such as the inland schists and granites, large blood-red garnet crystals that originated in diamond pipes and are suitable for cutting, faceting and polishing are found on the Skeleton Coast, usually in the same marine terraces as diamonds. More interesting in this connection, however, is the fine garnet sand which occurs sporadically along the beaches, covering long stretches in washes of dark maroon. The same garnet sand also blows into the dune areas, where, because of its higher specific gravity in relation to the quartz grains of the main dune bodies, it forms a bright coating on the backs of dunes and intriguing patterns down their slipfaces. A striking example of garnet-coated dunes is the colourful dune-belt behind Terrace Bay.

Two black minerals which are frequently seen in association with the fine garnet sand are magnetite and ilmenite. The tiny particles of magnetite, which adhere to a magnet when brought close enough, are a form of iron ore. Ilmenite consists of iron oxide and titanium. These minerals are often seen in association with garnet crystals as dune coatings, in colourfully surreal patterns down the slipfaces. A particularly striking occurrence of magnetite and ilmenite is often seen on the backs of shrub-coppice dunes when the black mineral particles combine with light yellow quartz granules in starkly graphic arrangements of zebra-like stripes.

A metal which has thus far evaded prospectors in so far as the discovery of a major ore body is concerned, but of which traces nevertheless occur in various forms all along the coast as well as further inland, is copper. Various shades of green copper-oxide contained in a variety of stones and rocks can be seen at a large number of locations. A fairly substantial uranium deposit has been discovered in the Engo Valley north of Angra Fria. Compared to the uranium deposits in the vicinity of Swakopmund, however, the deposit is relatively small and, owing to a lack of any proper infrastructure, does not justify exploitation.

Despite the Skeleton Coast's superficial resemblance to the oil-producing deserts of Saudi Arabia, Iraq and Iran, geologists are in agreement that it is extremely unlikely that there is any oil on the Skeleton Coast, because of the tremendous volcanic action that took place 120 million years ago. The heat and movement of such action would have destroyed whatever oil deposits may have existed in the area. Anthracite coal was located by drilling just north of the Huab River, but at such a great depth that mining it at that stage was not a proposition. Thin, very low-grade coal also occurs in the vicinity of Orupembe, east of Angra Fria and near the Doros Crater.

Another discovery which at the time caused considerable excitement was that of large iron-ore deposits at Ongaba and Ovihende in Kaokoland. This find was thoroughly prospected by the Bethlehem Steel Corporation. However, owing to the lack of infrastructure and the relatively low grade, a mine was never developed. A subsequent discovery of larger and better iron-ore deposits at Sishen in the Republic of South Africa has considerably diminished the importance and attractiveness of the Kaokoland deposits.

SALT-PANS

Salt-pans occur sporadically all the way up the coast. The largest and better-known ones are at Cape Cross, where rock salt is mined, the Huab and Koichab salt-pans and the large Cape Frio brine-pan complex. The latter covers an extensive area approximately 90 km in length and varies in width from a few metres to several kilometres. Although a certain amount of rock salt is found mostly around the edges, these pans contain mainly a mixture of sand and highly concentrated brine of which the salt content comprises between 25 and 28 per cent; this is the concentration at which water becomes sufficiently saturated for salt crystals to form. Geophysical surveys at Angra Fria have revealed that some of these brine pans are over 100 m deep and experts maintain that enormous quantities of high-quality salt could be produced for an unlimited period of time by simply pumping the water out of the pans and allowing it to crystallise. Unfortunately, salt is a low-price commodity and consequently, although the salt thus produced would be very inexpensive, the transportation costs to the various world markets would prevent such an undertaking from becoming economically viable. Less is known of the Huab and Koichab salt-pans. They are cut off from the sea and are believed to contain relatively large quantities of rock salt. The Cape Cross salt-pans on the other hand have been extensively researched and prospected. Drilling has revealed that solid rock salt occurs in certain places to depths of 25 m.

WHITE CLAY CASTLES

An interesting geological feature of the Skeleton Coast is the so-called white 'temples' or 'castles', impressive formations of whitish-yellow sedimentary clay which occur in the Hoarusib Canyon. These formations, which also occur at Homeb in the Kuiseb River near Walvis Bay, are the remnants of ancient river silt deposits. They have been ascribed by some geomorphologists to the damming up of the river behind the dunes less than a million years ago. Others consider them to be simply thick flood-plain deposits during a period of less active downward erosion. The dune-damming process is currently in evidence at the lower reaches

Overleaf

6 Springbok at the mouth of the Hoarusib River with the Atlantic Ocean in the background. The Skeleton Coast is one of the few places in the world today where springbok, and even lion, are seen on the beaches.

7 The lucrative man-made guano platforms of Cape Cross, generally regarded as the southernmost point of the Skeleton Coast. These bird platforms have a surface area close on 70 000 square metres and attract seabirds, mainly cormorants, in vast numbers. The guano is 'reaped' annually.

27

6

7

8

9

of the Hoanib River. Cut off from the sea by the dune belt which runs parallel to the coast from Torra Bay to the Kunene, the river has formed a large flood-plain consisting of deposits of the same kind of fine silt. The Hoarusib River broke through to the sea again at a later stage, and the silt formations were gradually eroded by water and wind to their present form of pillars and columns. Whatever their origin, they lend an exotic touch to the Hoarusib Canyon and, with the odd clump of makalani palms, transport one momentarily to the pyramids and palm trees of Egypt.

THE BEACHES

The beaches of the Skeleton Coast are either rocky, sandy or covered in pebbles. As a general rule it can be said that where the inland rock formations consist of granite and gneiss, the beaches and storm terraces tend to be sandy. Where on the other hand the beaches are bordered by lavas and basalts they tend to be stony, while the storm terraces consist of oblong pebbles. Samples of just about every single stone that occurs in the Skeleton Coast and its hinterland seem to have concentrated on the pebble beaches, particularly at Möwe Bay. Rounded and smoothed by wave action, a cornucopia of colour is washed up onto the beach in the form of granite, basalt, sandstone, agate, cornelian and quartz, in every conceivable shade of the geological rainbow.

DUNE FORMATIONS

Sprawled like massive pieces of modern sculpture over its surface, dunes are a living and integral part of the desert. In an ever-changing cosmos of colour and contour they roar and rumble, smoke and wander. Far more than mere heaps of sand, dunes are shaped the way they are for very specific reasons. Formed by the deposition of sand by wind, the size, shape and pattern of the dune depend on the availability and grain size of the sand in relation to the direction, speed and turbulence of the wind. A normal dune initially takes shape on the leeward side of an obstruction and any stone or bush can be the original point around which it is built. It could also start forming around a mound of sand which has been dropped during a lull in a sand-transporting wind.

A normal dune has a long backslope on the windward side and a shorter, steeper downwind slope, called the leeside or slipface. When the slipface reaches its maximum angle of repose, gravitational pull causes the sand to slip down. All dunes move to a greater or lesser extent. Even the very large dunes, which by virtue of their size have apparently stabilised, also move, although very slowly. For all practical purposes shrub-coppice dunes stabilise around vegetation, whereas the transitory barchan dunes 'migrate' and travel from between 3 to 15 m a year. In the latter case sand particles are picked up by the wind from the long gradual backslope and dropped over the steep foreslope, so that the dune moves downwind.

These regular and repeated sand patterns caused by wind occur in three groups, namely, ripples, dunes and draa. A draa is an outsized dune of which the windward and leeward faces are often covered with smaller dunes. Draa, like single dunes and ripples, are regularly spaced and patterned. These three have a hierarchical arrangement in that ripples are nearly always superimposed on the

Previous page

8   A typical coastal landscape with basalt and granite outcrops and characteristic barchan dune. Barchan dunes are crescent-shaped, the result of unidirectional winds blowing the sand more readily over the low tips of the dune than over its centre, and form where sand is relatively scarce.

9   A dried-out tuft of grass, remnant of a forgotten desert shower, clings tenaciously to the desert surface.

backs of dunes, while dunes are commonly found superimposed on the backs of draa, all three the result of the interplay of wind and sand.

The dunes of the Skeleton Coast are the result of wind deposition of sand churned out onto the beaches by Atlantic waves and seized by the prevailing south and south-west winds. Where longitudinal dunes stretch parallel to the prevailing wind direction, transverse dunes lie across the path of the wind, like waves in an ocean, while oblique dunes are divergent or slanting in relation to the wind. Along the coast where the prevailing south-west wind is very strong the dunes are formed transversely. Starting at Torra Bay and running through to Rocky Point is a belt of tightly knit transverse dunes. These dunes are clearly genetically linked to barchans. From Rocky Point further northwards regular concentrations of barchan dunes occur all the way up the coast, changing back to a belt of transverse dunes just before and up to the Kunene River. Adjacent to these coastal dune belts are sporadic occurrences of longitudinal dunes. The other dune formation commonly seen is the shrub-coppice, knob or hump dune which occurs near the coast, in river-beds and on inland plains.

The Transitory Barchan Dune

Visually one of the most captivating of dune formations is the barchan, a crescent-shaped dune which forms where sand is relatively scarce. The shape results from a unidirectional wind blowing the sand more readily over the low

Overleaf

10   The wastes of the remote and lonely Engo Valley are coloured pink by feldspar gravel eroded from the surrounding granitic gneiss formations.

11

12

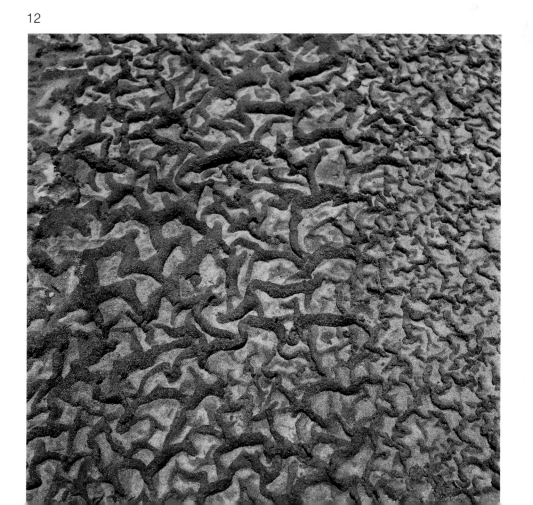

tips of the dune than over its centre. These dunes occur in various other parts of the world such as Peru, Algeria, Arabia, Niger and around the Persian Gulf, with differences in size and shape and development of oblique elements. Characteristic of the barchans of the Skeleton Coast are the pronounced scallops on the inside of the half-moon-shaped crest before the arms start tapering down. As they are formed by the prevailing south-west winds they all point north-east. The western arm is always more elongated than the eastern arm, for all practical purposes pointing in the direction in which the barchan is travelling. The reason why the western arm is longer than the eastern arm is attributed to an asymmetry in the wind pattern, an asymmetry in the sand supply, or to a slope in the desert surface.

These dunes are the most transitory of the migrating dunes and move visibly with speeds which average between 2 and 3 m a year, in some areas up to 15 m a year, covering and uncovering whatever crosses their path. The popular name 'wandering dune' is therefore misleading, as the travelling barchan invariably moves in the same direction. Between Torra Bay and Terrace Bay there is an unusually colourful stretch of what could possibly be termed chains of linked-up barchan dunes. Sufficient sand supply has enabled them to coalesce into complicated asymmetrical patterns. The windward sides of the dunes are coated with a maroon layer of fine garnet crystals which is heavier than the yellow quartz grains that constitute the body of the dune. The winding black 'streets' in between the dune reticule consist of hard basaltic lava or its gravelly products of erosion.

A strange phenomenon that is prevalent in certain dunes, and is a feature of many of the larger barchans, is that under given circumstances they make a rumbling or roaring sound. When the build up of sand on the crest reaches the point that gravitational pull causes it to slide down the slipface, the dune 'roars'. The upshot of several theories as to why this happens is that because the sand grains are extremely dry and have no capillary water whatsoever, they produce noises of varying pitch and volume caused by friction between the grains as they cascade down the slipface, rather like a small avalanche. Whether the noise is the result of the grains moving against each other, or possibly of static electricity produced by this friction, the rumbling sound is amplified in the crescent-shaped 'amphitheatre' of the dune, the loudest sound coming from the centre. It is also evident that the warmer and drier the dune, the greater the propensity it has to 'roar', and the larger the dune, the greater the amplification as it 'roars'. The geological components underlying the dune also play a role in determining the extent to which the sound waves are reverberated back into the dune. Dunes situated on granite formations, for instance, tend to produce a louder rumbling sound than on others.

Shrub-coppice Dunes

Shrub-coppice dunes are a familiar sight, especially near the coast and in dry river courses. They are relatively small, on average up to one or two metres high, and have a rounded hump-like shape which sometimes trails off for one or two metres, generally in the same direction as the prevailing wind. They are, in effect, mounds of sand which have accumulated around vegetation. Those on the coast most commonly host the nondescript but nutritious, salt-tolerant brack-bush, whereas larger ones form around narra bushes, usually in dry and ancient river courses where the long tap-root of the narra can reach supplies of subterranean water. The mat of continuous vegetation provides the ideal sand-stabilising agent: the root system holds together the underlying sand, the superstructure decreases the wind velocity, and wind-blown sand grains lodge among the stems and leaves.

Cascading sand caused by a passing gemsbok creates new patterns on a sandy bank.

By extending its root system the plant continues to survive at the top as the mound becomes larger.

Shrub-coppice dunes occur in two categories. The small sand-streaming variety occurs near the coast in exposed areas and has a banner-like ridge, which can reach lengths of several metres before tapering off. These comparatively attractive dunes are generally composed of firmly compacted coarse sand. Less attractive are the sand knobs, elephant head or knob dunes which are mainly accumulations of sand around dune lucerne, dollar bushes and tufts of perennial grass. These dunes can build up to a height of 5 m and may eventually transform themselves into laterally spreading transverse dunes.

Longitudinal Dunes and Ripples

Longitudinal dunes, which cover the largest area of the central Namib dune-sea, are relatively scarce in the Skeleton Coast section of the Namib. They occur sporadically 20 to 30 km inland from the Hoanib up to the Kunene River, lying more or less in a north–south direction. A cross-section of one of these dunes would be asymmetrical. The north–south crest is sharply defined, the western slope is steep, narrow and relatively uniform, whereas the eastern slope is wider, more gradual and more complex.

In some ways even more intriguing than dune formations are ripple patterns, which give texture, a graphic quality and colour to the windward sides of dunes, dune streets and flat desert surfaces. There is nothing simple, incidental or haphazard about the way the many varieties of ripple continua form, in which complicated rather than simple patterns are the rule. Other than variations in wind strength and flow patterns, it seems that the main factors which determine the degree of rippling are the amounts of sand available, the variation in size and specific gravity of the grains and the combination of types of sand and gravel. It also seems that rippling is more likely to occur where the sand is a mixture of fine and coarser grains, in which case the patterns become particularly complex and striking.

Overleaf
13   A rugged landscape of gneiss and pink granite veinlets near Angra Fria.

14   Although tracks in sand usually disappear quite rapidly, on the gravel plains the damage is virtually irreparable and according to experts could take up to a thousand years to mend.

13

14

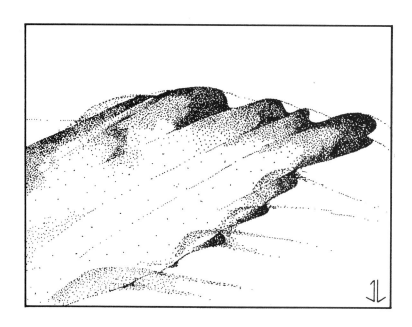

The Climate

... conditions that create a unique desert ecosystem

Previous page

15   Cloud and shadow play
over a loose reticule of
barchan dunes. These dunes,
often referred to as wandering
dunes, are transitory and
move from three to fifteen
metres a year, depending on
their size and location. In the
Namib barchans always travel
in a north/north-easterly
direction.

THE SKELETON COAST as we know it today is very much the product of its climate. The dense coastal fogs and cold sea breezes caused by the ice-cold Benguela Current and the hot bergwinds from the interior generate both its singular ecosystem and its aura of mystery and impenetrability. Paradoxically, it has one of the most humid atmospheres in the world, but the layer of moist air is very thin and does not contain sufficient moisture to cause rainfall. The coast is pleasantly cool throughout the year, except on those days during the winter months when bergwinds blow and then temperatures higher than those in summer are often recorded. Inland temperatures rise sharply during the day because the interior is not subject to the cooling influence of the Benguela Current. There are three other areas in the world with climates comparable to that of the Namib: the northern Chilean coast; the western coast of the Mexican State of Baja California; and the western coast of Australia. These three coastal deserts have basically the same setting as the Namib in that they are all on the western coast of a continent, are adjacent to a cold sea and have a tropic running through them.

One hundred and twenty million years ago, when West Gondwanaland began to break away, a narrow strip of coast was formed, bordered to the west by the South Atlantic Ocean and to the east by a mountainous escarpment. This tract of land, some 2000 km long and 100 km wide, was destined to become the Namib Desert of today. Contrary to the established belief that initial desertification was caused by the effects of the cold Benguela Current after it had started flowing up the west coast of Namibia, evidence now suggests that, for the past 80 million years, the area which today comprises the Namib Desert experienced semi-arid to arid conditions long before the full establishment of the Benguela Current system approximately six million years ago. Additional evidence

A waterfall of sand cascades over 20 m down a sheer rock face into the dry bed of the Hoarusib Canyon.

suggests that a predominantly southerly wind system similar to that of today deposited the sand seas of the central and southern Namib at least 65 million years ago, also long before the development of the present Benguela Current system. Especially interesting are fossil finds which imply that warm water conditions once existed in the south Atlantic Ocean, in contrast with the situation today. It was, therefore, considerably *after* initial desertification had set in that the cold water of the Benguela Current was gradually directed up along the west coast of Southern Africa by winds caused by pressure systems approaching from the west and south-west, and that its cooling and upwelling features began to play a major role in the further aridification of the Namib.

THE BENGUELA CURRENT AND THE COASTAL FOG

The Benguela Current, prime determinant of the essential character of the

Overleaf

16   A hot and sometimes exceedingly unpleasant bergwind, referred to in Namibia as the **Ostwind,** blows during the winter months, often causing higher temperatures than those normally recorded in summer. Here it is literally blowing the surf backwards into the sea.

Namib Desert and Skeleton Coast today, flows from Antarctica towards the southernmost tip of Africa, from where it is directed up the west coast as far as Mossamedes on the Angolan coast. Here it turns west and merges with a warm equatorial current which flows towards South America. An interesting and influential feature of the Benguela Current is that the temperatures of the water next to the coast are always lower than further out in the ocean. The reason for this is that the outside arc of the current is the side that flows closest to Antarctica and eventually up the west coast of Namibia. Temperatures next to the coast are generally in the region of 12° C to 15° C, while further out at sea they are between 18° C and 20° C, which causes both the evaporation rate and the air temperatures out at sea to be higher than those closer to the shore. When this relatively warmer and more moist air flows towards the coast and rises because of the elevation of the land, the resultant mixture of two air masses with different temperatures causes condensation and advective fog is formed.

This virtually omnipresent coastal fog, which hangs suspended as a dense belt over the ocean near the coast on most days, is a particularly characteristic feature of the Skeleton Coast. Because of this, for about 340 days of the year the atmosphere at the coast is extremely damp, the humidity on most days more than 90 per cent, often reaching 100 per cent. During the night when the desert surface cools, the invisible, humid sea air of the day is transformed into visible clouds of mist as a result of condensation, or, as it is usually formulated, the fog moves in towards the interior. This happens for the first 50 km inland on about two days out of three, less often further toward the interior, although the fog sometimes penetrates as far as 100 km on up to 60 days a year. In the low-lying river courses the penetration is much deeper than on the more elevated gravel plains. Here and on the beaches it often lies suspended as a low cloud between 200 to 400 m above the ground, whereas on higher ground it rests on the surface, sometimes leading to a fine drizzle in the early mornings. This explains why the lichen fields on the more elevated plains bloom so luxuriantly on certain mornings. This early mist creates an eerie atmosphere in which sounds tend to be muffled and hushed and vegetation and dunes appear disproportionately large and out of focus.

As the sun ascends in the sky the fog blanket warms up, heat rays penetrate and warm the ground surface, the warmed surface radiates heat rays and the mist 'lifts' and disperses. The fine water droplets which condensed during the night and emerged as fog in the early morning are sufficiently heated to change back to transparent molecules of water vapour. This 'invisible' vapour can often be seen as a hazy belt along the coast when approaching from the interior by air, and on certain days causes the sun to seem less 'potent' at the coast than further inland. As the day progresses a sea breeze begins to blow, which gradually increases in strength and disperses the remaining moisture and vapour over the desert.

RAINFALL AND TEMPERATURES

The prevailing sea breeze from the Atlantic is too cold and stable for sufficient rain-cloud formation, factors which, combined with the latitude around the tropic of Capricorn, result in a dry, high-pressure region with strong downward atmospheric currents. The upwelling of cold water from the depths near the shore caused by winds and the continental shelf, further maintain a low temperature on the surface of the current. The steep climatic gradient, that is, the sudden drop in annual rainfall in the desert as compared to that of the adjacent escarpment, is, however, only partly attributable to the presence of the Benguela Current and its associated upwelling. Additional factors are the high-pressure system of the south Atlantic anticyclone, the location of the Namib in the rainshadow below the western Namibian escarpment, and the fact that the summer rains which fall in the interior hardly ever reach the coast. These rains are the last deposits of moisture taken up by north and north-west winds over the warm Agulhas Current as it flows down the east coast of Africa. By the time the winds reach the Namibian escarpment after a westerly movement over thousands of kilometres, they are mostly devoid of rain. When they descend the escarpment such moisture as they might still have tends to evaporate before it can reach the ground in the form of rain, because of the warm dry air over the desert.

Annual rainfall figures for the Skeleton Coast are between 15 and 25 mm. Rain falls in three or four separate showers in different locations in different years, and is often not much more than a slight drizzle. Heavy downpours are rare and tend to occur further inland. The occasional coastal thundershower or rain usually comes from cut-off low-pressure systems near the coast which have originated from low-pressure systems over the mid-Atlantic south-west of Cape Town. The cold air over the ocean converges with relatively warm air from the interior, producing light rainshowers of between one and six millimetres.

Contrary to a popular belief that the Skeleton Coast can become unpleasantly hot, especially during the summer months, temperatures are relatively cool and moderate, and rarely exceed 30° C. Indeed, the differences between

Overleaf
17   Mirages are a familiar sight on the Skeleton Coast and make for absorbing photography. These optical illusions are caused by the refraction of light passing through layers of atmosphere of varying density.

When on the rare occasion it does rain, 'barren' plains come to life within days as grass cover appears, apparently from nowhere.

18

19

Previous page

18   Breaking through a heavy build-up of thundercloud, the sun lights up a gnarled **omumborumbonga** or leadwood tree, **Combretum imberbe**. The wood of these trees is extremely hard and sinks to the bottom when immersed in water.

19   When it is particularly dry in the interior many gemsbok and springbok move into the desert and the lions have a 'roaring' time. The rains in 1982 in north-western Damaraland and Kaokoland caused many of these animals to move back into the interior, forcing the lions to resort to catching seals on the beach to stay alive.

summer and winter temperatures are not great and, paradoxically, the highest temperatures — up to 40° C and more, which are caused by bergwinds — are recorded during the winter. On the other hand, considerable fluctuations between day and night temperatures do sometimes occur in the desert proper, ranging from below freezing point at night to 42° C at midday. These fluctuations stem from the prevailing south and south-west winds blowing inland over a cold ocean, whereas north and east winds from the interior are warm. As a rule, however, the climate is pleasant, well balanced and refreshing.

THE WINDS

The prevailing winds at the coast are the south and south-west winds which blow throughout the year, on some occasions as pleasant and refreshing breezes, on others as vicious and relentless gales which reach speeds of up to 50 km an hour. These winds are produced by the high-pressure system which exists more or less permanently over the southern Atlantic Ocean and from which air flows towards the relatively low-pressure areas at the coast. Because of the stability of the air, low evaporation and rapid condensation, the west winds bring no rain. They do, however, play a major role in the formation of the landscape, for they catch up the sand which is washed up on the shores by the tide, transporting and

Sand-blasted by the strong coastal winds are bleached bones left by ruthless whalers of the previous century, all that remains of the once prolific whale population which inhabited the plankton-rich waters off the Skeleton Coast.

A thin layer of dried silt, eroded by the winds, gradually being engulfed by sand.

depositing it as dunes further inland. They largely determine the shape of the dunes and, in the case of barchans, the direction in which they move. Except for short periods during winter when east wind conditions prevail, the slipfaces on the coastal dunes face north.

A wind which has a strong impact on the character of the Skeleton Coast is the infamous *Ostwind*, a typical bergwind which blows mainly from April to July, the transition period between summer and winter. It is this wind that brings the life-giving detritus from the interior as food supplies for the many small and uniquely adapted creatures of the dunes. The bergwinds originate from a high-pressure system over the interior of Southern Africa, a high-pressure system in the upper stratum causing subsiding air, and a coastal low which starts in Angola north of the Kunene River and moves down south, so that the air flows anti-clockwise over the interior from east to west. This relatively cool air starts off on the eastern side of Southern Africa as a cool breeze which warms up as it loses moisture and converges over the interior plateau. When it descends the western escarpment towards the coast, the air diverges and becomes even warmer. For every 100 m that it loses height, it gains 1° C in temperature, from the compression caused by the increase in air pressure. It is further warmed by the heat of the desert and can reach temperatures of up to 40° C and more. By the time it reaches the coast it is hot, dry and exceedingly unpleasant.

Overleaf
20 Cape cormorants, as much part of the beaches as the pebbles, thrive on the rich pelagic off-shore resources of the cold Benguela Current. These birds are the main producers of guano. Many of the early explorations were embarked upon in order to establish the occurrence and economic viability of guano deposits along the coast.

The *Ostwind* usually blows intermittently for about a week, sometimes longer, gradually losing velocity. It starts early in the morning and normally persists until early afternoon, when, as temperatures over the interior reach their maximum and the airflow is cut off, it will die down very suddenly, leaving the air crystal clear. This clarity is the result of subsiding air caused by a high-pressure system in the upper layers of the atmosphere, which prevents the dust from rising from the surface. A cool sea breeze wafts across the land almost immediately and the sound of the breakers, which has been drowned out by the *Ostwind*, becomes audible again. As is often the case with bergwinds, the *Ostwind* has a pronounced psychological effect on people. In Germany statistics have shown that suicide rates escalate when the bergwinds blow. The dampening effects of the *Ostwind* lift miraculously when it retreats and the cool oxygen-laden west wind blows in from the ocean.

SULPHUR ERUPTIONS

The sub-oceanic mountain ridge, which runs in a south-westerly direction from more or less north of Angra Fria towards South America, forms a basin or 'trap' for the many minerals and plankton brought up from Antarctica by the Benguela Current. This makes the waters off the Skeleton Coast particularly rich in plankton or 'nutrient soup' and accounts for their importance as fish-breeding grounds. The basin also causes the plankton and minerals to well up to the surface, which is why plankton foam is so often seen on the Skeleton Coast, washed to shore as a thick creamy foam after being churned up by the waves when the sea is rough. It collects in huge quivering heaps up to a metre or more high which the wind blows apart and sends scudding over the smooth wet beaches like self-automated hovercrafts and up onto the dry sand. When it dries out, it turns into dirty-looking splotches of khaki-green scum.

When plankton dies in the ocean it sinks to the bottom and collects in traps on the seabed, where it becomes covered in fine, heavy mud. Under this mud the dead plankton rots and starts releasing gases, a process which speeds up when temperatures rise. These gases eventually 'explode' and rise to the surface, releasing bubbles of sulphur which can on occasion be smelt for several kilometres inland. Sometimes the mud covering under which the rotting process takes places is also brought up by the bubbles and floats on the surface like small flat islands. From the air these eruptions can be seen as large clear patches of turquoise in the otherwise dark and murky water. Dead fish, poisoned by the sulphurous gases, are sometimes washed up onto the beaches when the eruptions occur. Just how potent is this released sulphur can be seen from the way it affects the paintwork of houses at the coast: greyish-black splotches, almost like burnt patches, appear on the wooden surfaces.

MIRAGES

Mirages are very much part of the desert experience. The images of elongated ostriches walking over shimmering sheets of water, inverted inselbergs and ethereal chains of islands floating above the horizon, are real enough to record photographically, but they retain an elusive distance from the observer by receding or simply disappearing altogether when approached.

On several of the early maps of the Skeleton Coast bays were marked which apparently do not exist. It is quite possible that the Viktoria Augusta Harbour, a bay 'discovered' by the jurist, Dr Esser, but never located by subsequent explorers, was nothing more than a mirage, observed on a calm day from the sea looking towards a flat stretch of beach, when the temperatures of the different layers of the atmosphere were conducive to the creation of the image of a bay. It is also conceivable that some of the many sailing ships which ran aground along the Skeleton Coast did so because they approached shore towards such a 'bay' and, realising too late that the goal was an illusion, were driven onto a hidden reef by the strong current and south-west wind. This in turn conjures up visions of footsore and thirsty castaways, staggering across flat desert plains towards those ever-receding expanses of water.

A mirage is in fact an optical illusion caused by the refraction of light as it passes through layers of atmosphere of varying density. The atmosphere acts as a giant lens, bending the light rays that come through it. Objects in the distance may be raised above or depressed below their normal position and are often distorted into irregular and fantastic shapes. Although many of the images look as if they are reflections in irregular mirrors, reflection plays no part in the formation of a mirage. An apparent water surface is really an image of the sky and objects such as mountains which appear to be reflected in this surface, are actually refracted versions of the original object, not reflected ones. If the observer were to kneel down, the surfaces would terminate much closer, or if on the other hand he were to go higher up, the whole mirage might disappear.

There are several kinds of mirages, of which the inferior or lower mirage occurs on the Skeleton Coast. These mirages, also called two-image mirages, are usually associated with deserts. The distant, nearly level, desert surface assumes the appearance of a sheet of water, which is in effect a second inverted image of the sky as observed from a slight elevation, or from a point above the heated layer of air. This is the same kind of mirage that is seen over a hot tarred road. The air over a hot surface of land lies in layers, with the hottest and least dense layers below and closest to the ground. The index of refraction depends mainly on the temperature. A high temperature results in low density and a low index of refraction. The stronger the temperature gradient, that is, the greater the change of temperature with distance, the greater the change of the index of refraction with distance. As the observer moves backwards and forwards, so does the optical horizon, as would the 'water' on a road surface advance and recede if the driver were to drive backwards and forwards on the road.

When the mirage is witnessed over a flat desert plain, trees, rocks and other landscape features are inverted, that is, they appear in the sky upside down, and there might also be an upright image of the same object above the inverted one. When the object is a gemsbok or ostrich it makes for a truly spectacular mirage.

Superior or upper mirages are usually described in connection with water surfaces and mostly in association with colder atmospheres where there is a strong temperature inversion, with warm layers of air above cooler layers. The images in superior mirages are also more clearly defined than in inferior mirages. In the latter case shimmering is typical and is caused by small irregularities in density and temperature that result from turbulence in the air.

Visitors to the Skeleton Coast, generally those who come from the colder countries, sometimes refer to the mirages as fata Morganas. The fata Morgana is, however, a far more complicated type of mirage than the variety that generally occurs in deserts. In a fata Morgana the transformation is so great that it bears no resemblance to the object that caused it. Dark mountain ranges, towering castles,

Overleaf
22 Black granite inselbergs float in the shimmering glimmer of a midday mirage.

23 The brightly coloured flower of the Bushman's candle, **Sarcocaulon mossamedense**. The dried-out resinous bark gives off a pleasant smell when burnt and is sometimes used as incense.

24 On reaching the maximum angle of repose the sand cascades down, as if through an hourglass.

51

22

23

24

25

26

pilasters and arches built like those of Roman aqueducts are described and these are usually observed on water surfaces and in colder atmospheres. Under ostwind conditions this kind of mirage is sometimes seen at the Skeleton Coast.

Another optical illusion typical of the Skeleton Coast is the varying shapes that the sun assumes at different times of day. Through the early morning mist it looks like a flat, well-defined moon. As it sinks over the ocean to the western horizon it is distorted by the low-lying layer of moisture and changes shape through the coastal mist from a flat, oval disc to an hourglass in various stages and finally, to a brilliantly coloured globular sphere, before disappearing suddenly and without ceremony behind the dense bank of fog above the sea.

The Plants

. . . evolved to survive in a desert environment

UNLIKE THE REST of the country the Namib does not experience drought in the true sense of the word. Rainless conditions are the norm but, because the desert is kept moist by dew and dense morning fogs, fostered by the cold Benguela Current and blown in from the Atlantic Ocean during the night, an extraordinary plant community with a large number of endemic species has evolved. Subjected to extremes of temperature, strong winds and encroaching sands, these plants have ensured their survival by developing a wide spectrum of ingenious adaptations, which involves the acquisition, retention and storage of moisture. The vital life-giving fog is pushed 40 to 50 km inland, and creates a relatively cool and moist zone all the way up the coast. The effects of this regular supply of moisture are clearly illustrated by the substantial differences between the plant communities on the western slopes of mountains and ridges — against which the fog moisture is blown — and those on the eastern slopes. When on the rare occasion it does rain, 'barren' plains come to life within days with grass cover, a variety of succulents and new growths appearing as if from nowhere.

DUNE VEGETATION

Vegetation which grows in association with dunes is widely distributed through-

Overleaf

27   A quartet of gemsbok etched against a heavy bank of morning fog which has blown inland from the sea during the night.

out the Skeleton Coast. The most common plants are the ganna or brack-bush, narra, dollar-bush, desert parsley and dune lucerne. Ganna in particular provides valuable fodder for the animals of the desert, such as springbok, gemsbok, ostrich and many other birds and insects. Although these bushes appear to grow on top of the dunes, it is the other way round: the dune develops or 'grows' around the bush, a formation which is called a shrub-coppice, hump or knob dune. The young plant causes an initial build-up of sand on the downwind side. As the mound becomes larger it gradually links up with the plant, which continues to grow at the top by extending its root system.

Two species of ganna or brack-bush occur at the Skeleton Coast: *Salsola aphylla*, which grows mainly in river-beds; and the larger and more commonly seen coastal ganna or brack-bush, *Salsola nollothensis*, which grows in association with a dune. The fact that a dune forms around it to a large extent ensures its survival. The sand serves not only as an anchor against the strong prevailing winds, but also as a sponge, which absorbs and retains the fog and morning dew and enables its roots to obtain sufficient moisture for the plant to put out new shoots all year round.

Coastal ganna are straggly, untidy and rather nondescript bushes. The small, crumbly, dusky grey-green leaves are, however, highly nutritious. The seeds, which look like small dried-out flowers, are very attractive when looked at through a magnifying glass, while the leaves are small, round, fleshy, and covered with fine grey hairs. Apparently, ganna can also absorb water through its leaves. When the bush has been enveloped by fog for any length of time, the leaf surface expands in the same way that the skin on one's hands stretches and wrinkles when immersed in water for a while. The resultant difference in pressure inside and on the outside of the leaf causes the moisture which has precipitated on the leaf surface to be drawn inwards. Ganna dunes do not grow much higher than one or two metres. They sometimes tend to converge and develop into large bumpy, compound dunes, causing the roots to go down fairly deep.

Whereas the ganna is dependent on fog for survival and grows virtually all along the coast, narra plants grow in the vicinity of present and old river courses, where their roots can reach subterranean water. They therefore have a wider distribution towards the interior. Narra dunes tend to be considerably higher than ganna dunes. In exceptional cases they reach heights of up to 20 m, with tap-roots up to 20 cm in diameter which grow 15 or more metres deep.

The narra plant, *Acanthosicyos horrida*, which is endemic to the Namib, and its close relative, the well-known tsama, *Citrullus lanatus*, are the ancestors of melons and watermelons. With its bright green slender stems and spindly thorns the narra is a far more attractive plant than the ganna. The *horrida* part of its scientific name means that instead of leaves the plant has paired thorns, which grow up to 4 cm long. Photosynthesis takes place directly through the stem. The plant has wax-like, greenish-white blossoms and the fruit is round and spiny and especially favoured by porcupine, hyaena and gemsbok for its watery sap.

Hottentots and Bushmen, who in earlier years frequented the Skeleton Coast, and the Topnaars, a Hottentot clan which settled in the Kuiseb River bed many years ago and still lives there in isolated settlements, evolved an unusual culture round the narra. The flesh of the fruit is used in many different ways. Although the sap has an unpalatable taste, it is potable and sometimes used, once it has been expressed from the pulp, to make a kind of beer. The pulp that remains can be prepared in several ways. It can be baked into a kind of cake, or it can be cooked in a pot over a fire and, after straining off the seeds, poured onto clean sand to dry. After a few days the 'cake' is turned over so that the oil can

drain out of the other side. When it is dry, it is cut into strips, rolled up, and eaten as a sweet that is licked rather than chewed because of the sand adhering to it. In this form it can be kept for up to two years. The taste is rather neutral, nothing as piquant as that of the seeds. The latter have several uses and are generally considered a great delicacy. Once separated from the flesh, they are put out to dry. Roasted and salted like peanuts, they are extremely tasty. They can also be ground to a pulp which looks and tastes rather like marzipan. The Topnaars eat this extremely rich substance with porridge. During the war years when almonds were unobtainable, narra paste was used as a substitute for marzipan. Narra pips are highly nutritious: they contain 57 per cent oil, which has a high percentage of polyunsaturated fatty acid, and 31 per cent protein, as well as fair amounts of iron, kalium, magnesium and phosphorus, ideal for people with high cholesterol counts.

Another plant which grows in association with a dune is the so-called dollar-bush, *Zygophyllum stapfii*. It sometimes occurs on plains where the sand tends to be transitory, the dunes often no more than slight humps. Its characteristic round, flat and shiny, coin-like leaves give rise to its name. They are a bright and luxuriant green which makes the dollar-bush an extremely attractive plant and lightens up an otherwise colourless plain. When the leaves turn yellow, the plant dies and the wood of the stem dries into fantastically gnarled shapes. The dried,

The prickly fruit of the narra plant, **Acanthosicyos horrida,** is edible and much favoured by gemsbok. The pips have an extremely high nutritional value and can be ground to a paste in taste and texture rather like marzipan.

Overleaf

28   The seal colony at Cape Frio has grown steadily in recent years and numbers an estimated 20 000. These seals are not culled like the seals of Cape Cross.

Previous page
29 The holy ancestral fire of
the Himba is kept alive by the
oldest member of a family.
This old man fell asleep next
to such a fire and was blinded
and disfigured by the flames
when his blankets caught
alight. In accordance with
Himba tradition he is now
cared for by his relatives.

naturally sculptured wood is very hard, of a rich reddish-brown colour, and when lying on exposed plains is polished by the wind and sand to a smooth and satiny gloss.

Dune parsley, *Merremia guerichii*, which looks rather like a white morning-glory creeper, is a prostrate, sprawling and picturesque vine, which tends to grow in association with low spreading dunes in gravelly areas. The flowers are white or light yellow, sometimes with a maroon centre, and the small clustered leaves, which resemble sprigs of parsley, and slender stems are dark green. The stems invariably develop runners and the plant spreads flatly in new directions, growing in a dense mat when the location is sufficiently protected, which looks like a miniature maze of avenues and boulevards, lined with small tufted trees.

Dune lucerne, *Hermannia gariepina*, on the other hand, grows straight upwards, also mainly in association with lowish dunes. It tends to grow in smallish clumps, the leaves and stalks are pale green, and the flowers, of which there are often more than there are leaves, are small and of a mauvish-blue colour.

GRASSES

A grass which appears in and on the dunes after it has rained is the tough annual, *Brachiaria psammophila*, known as zebra or gemsbok grass. The blades are bright green, short and very hairy. It grows in series of short transverse rows, facing the wind, and is typical of dune vegetation.

The short silvery shaving-brush grass, *Stipagrostis subacaulis*, also appears directly after the rains, mainly on gravel plains. Shaving-brush grass consists mainly of seed and will light up an entire plain with its glossy sheen. Large quantities of the seed are blown as detritus into the dune areas where they mass together in bright balls of silvery fluff serving as food stores for the insects and small mammals of the dunes.

Another grass of the gravel plains which appears directly after the rains is the fast-growing *Enneapogon desvauxii*, called the eight-day grass, because it reaches the flowering stage within eight days of germination. It grows in small, spread-out tufts, which often develop runners, sometimes spreading into dense mats. The inflorescence is a single, dense, ear-shaped plume. This grass never grows very high and is eaten mainly by smaller animals, especially springbok.

A grass not typical of the Namib but which occurs commonly in the western regions of Namibia, mostly in sandy areas, *Stipagrostis hochstetterana*, makes an occasional appearance at the Skeleton Coast, mostly on river banks and in dry river courses. This is the gemsbok tail grass, which can grow up to 1 metre in height, although it averages about 50 cm in desert areas. It is a perennial grass and grows in thick tufts. The conspicuous stiff white hairs on the awn are characteristic, while the inflorescence is a loosely flagged, silvery-white plume. It is extremely drought-resistant and even when dry has a high nutritional value.

Two species of quick-grass grow along the coast at river mouths where it tends to be damp. *Cynodon dactylon*, known as common quick-grass, and *Odyssea paucinervis* are very similar and can be distinguished only when in flower. Both are perennial, often have runners and can develop into dense mats. This type of grass is much favoured by springbok.

VELD VYGIES

Several species of *Mesembryanthemum*, or veld vygies, grow on the gravel flats close to the coast. Of these, *Mesembryanthemum cryptanthum*, descriptively called bleeding fingers, is typical of vegetation that appears shortly after a rain shower. It grows in vivid patches of green, red, yellow or orange, sprawling in all directions. It is an annual, low-growing plant with fat, swollen finger-like leaves which when squeezed seem to consist mainly of water, with very little fibre. The vygie most commonly seen in the desert is *Sesuvium sesuvioides* with its small purple, star-shaped flower. Through a magnifying glass the flower looks like an exotic orchid, hardly a tough xerophyte (that is, a plant adapted to dry conditions) existing marginally under harsh conditions. It grows in the most unlikely places, in crevices on barren granite rocks and on otherwise forsaken plains.

The ice-plant, *Mesembryanthemum guerichianum*, tends to grow on brackish soil. It has large, distinctive fleshy leaves with crystal-like, water-filled cells. After germination the young leaves are often red, but they gradually turn green as the plant matures. Animals are not partial to these plants, as they are very salty, which is probably why the ice-plant is also referred to as 'brack salad'. Another vygie commonly seen, usually in the coarser sand close to the coast, is *Psilocaulon kuntzei*, which has the erect beaded stem typical of *Psilocaulon* species. The small, delicate white flowers are perched on the tips of the stems, which never grow very high, at the most 30 cm. The fruit is bright red, and when seen through a magnifying glass looks like a ripe juicy strawberry.

RIVERINE VEGETATION

Many of the trees that occur along the dry river courses have grown from seed washed down from the interior when the rivers have come down in flood. Fed by subterranean water, they are not typical of desert vegetation, but are integral components of the ecosystem, as they provide food for the larger animals such as elephant, giraffe and rhino which roam up and down the dry river-beds. Incongruous and unexpected, bringing the tropics right into the desert, are the sporadic clumps of makalani palms, *Hyphaene ventricosa*, which occur along the Hoarusib River. The pips from which they originated were washed down from the far north-east, where makalani palms grow from Grootfontein northwards. They are slender and graceful trees and on average grow between 7 and 10 m high, in some localities up to 15 m. Makalani palms are dioecious, that is, there are separate male and female trees. The fruit is large and quite striking and while green and still soft, can be cooked and eaten. It ripens into a dark rich brown, while the shell becomes hard and smooth as if it has been polished. The outer part can be eaten and tastes rather like gingerbread. The kernel, referred to as vegetable ivory, is very hard and is used for carving ornaments. It is said that these palms can carry up to 2 000 nuts per tree per year. Elephants are very partial to the nuts, but more sought after than the fruit is the sap from the stem, which pushes out through the top. This sap tastes somewhat like ginger-beer and can be tapped by cutting off the tip of the palm. When the sap is left to ferment, it becomes an extremely potent alcoholic drink called palm wine. The Wambos, Kavangos and Bushmen all make use of makalani sap. It has been estimated that one such palm can be tapped for up to 70 litres, but with continual tapping will gradually die. Bushmen also utilise the young parts at the top of the trees as well as the marrow of the young stems, which they eat raw or cooked as a vegetable.

A tree which grows prolifically in the Hoarusib Canyon is the wild tamarisk, *Tamarix usneoides*, also somehow out of keeping with the surroundings, as it has

Overleaf

30 Despite expensive modern navigational equipment, the **Suiderkus** ran aground at Möwe Bay on her maiden voyage in December 1976. Battered by the waves, she gradually broke apart, the hull being deposited high on the beach one stormy night.

31

32

a vaguely pine-like appearance. It grows as a shrub or small to medium-sized tree and is an untidy-looking plant with dusky green leaves and small pink, white, grey or straw-coloured flowers. The tamarisk has an unusual way of keeping cool during the day. During the night a layer of salt on its leaves attracts moisture so that in the early morning the leaves are bright green. As the day progresses, the leaves turn a blue or grey-green from the crust of fine powdery salt that covers and protects them from excessive transpiration. This salt is easily rubbed off and is bitter to the taste. Elephants are particularly partial to tamarisk, which they trample mercilessly as they move up and down the canyon.

The mopane, *Colophospermum mopane*, a tree which is also restricted to the central areas of northern Namibia, grows in some of the river courses of the Skeleton Coast. With its elegant folded leaves, which resemble a pair of butterfly wings, it is a colourful and attractive tree. The new leaflets are bright red, turning into an almost luminescent green when they mature, yellow in autumn and finally, brown. During the heat of the day the leaves, which hang down, move closer together, causing hardly any shade at all. This is so as to expose a minimum of flat leaf surface to the sun. Mopane trees are an important food source for the larger animals and the dry pods which fall to the ground are also eaten. The latter smell strongly of turpentine.

Another conspicuous tree found along the river courses is the *omumborum-bonga* or leadwood tree, *Combretum imberbe*. For the Hereros the *omumborum-bonga* is a holy tree, believed to be the ancestor of all their peoples. It has a distinctive bark, smooth and grey and cracked in rectangular flakes. The leaves are small and grey-green, giving the whole tree a grey appearance. Most characteristic about this tree are the very long, twisted and gnarled roots which grow in fantastic contortions along the dry bed and banks of the river, to lengths of up to 50 m. The wood is heavy and extremely hard, so much so that it sinks to the bottom when immersed in water. Although not suitable for manufacturing furniture, it is ideal for making ornaments, as it turns well.

The most common and, in terms of fodder for game, the most valuable acacia which grows along the river courses is the ana tree, *Acacia albida*. It is Namibia's largest acacia and in a good year can yield up to one tonne of pods. The large nutritious pods have a high protein content and can be eaten by humans as well as animals. They are bright orange to reddish-brown and are very distinctive with their curled and twisted apple-ring shape. They drop from September to October, at a time when most other food has already been eaten, which makes the ana tree especially valuable. Another acacia which occurs in the river courses is the ubiquitous camel-thorn, *Acacia erioloba*. The bright yellow flowers, shaped like small puffy pompons, have a pungent and sweetish smell and the distinctive pod is creamy-grey and covered with fine velvety hairs.

The river green-thorn, *Balanites welwitschii*, grows mainly as a shrub. It has dark green leaves and thorns and an interesting oblong orange, sometimes yellow, fruit rather like a loquat, which has a sweet-sour taste and a very bitter after-taste. Elephants are very fond of this fruit. The mustard tree, *Salvadora persica*, is generally a low-growing and trailing shrub with rather fleshy, light to dark green, oblong leaves and fleshy spherical fruits which are pink to scarlet when mature. The fruit is edible and has an agreeable, aromatic taste, pungent and peppery.

Vegetation around waterholes, generally situated in the dry river courses, is comparatively luxurious and consists of a wealth of reeds, rushes and bulrushes. The mere sight of these unexpected splashes of green is almost thirst-quenching in itself. The poker plant or reed mace, *Typha capensis*, has an elongated inflorescence which is packed densely with brown seeds. When the seeds are ripe they break open into fluffy white wisps which drift away in the wind. *Phragmites australis,* commonly called *fluitjiesriet,* has hollow fluted stalks with large white, sometimes purple or mauve, plumes. *Scirpus littoralis* is an attractive upright reed with bright green stalks and reddish-brown tufted seeds on the ends.

Overleaf
33 A pastel mosaic of pink feldspar gravels and grey granite is sectioned by black dolerite dykes.

VEGETATION ON MOUNTAIN SLOPES AND ROCKY OUTCROPS

The vegetation which grows on mountain slopes and on rocky outcrops is in a sense the most interesting, as many of these plants have unusual adaptations. Because they are subjected to arid conditions, strong winds and extreme temperatures, they have assumed all sorts of weird and interesting shapes. One of the strangest of these is possibly the elephant's foot, *Adenia pechuelii,* which with its fat grey-green, thick-footed stem anchors itself by its tap-root firmly among rocks or in rock crevices. Its narrow herbaceous branches give it a hedgehog-like appearance and it almost seems ready to waddle off at the slightest provocation. It is hard to believe that this dry-looking, mostly leafless plant belongs to the *Granadilla* or passion-fruit family, Passifloraceae.

Another intriguing plant is the striking *Hoodia macrantha.* The large plate-like, reddish-brown flowers, which often grow in clusters, appear at the tops of thick, spiny and fleshy stems. These flowers with their purple hairs which are always in a state of quivering motion and their extremely unpleasant odour, somewhat resemble and smell like rotting meat. This is attractive to passing insects, which alight not only to drink the nectar but, in the case of the female, to lay eggs, in the belief that it is carrion. In the process they pick up pollen, which is then carried to the next flower. These plants are called *ghaap* (a Hottentot word meaning 'veld food') or *wildeghaap* and are eaten in their entirety by humans as well as animals, in particular black rhino, which might account for their relative scarcity. A genus which belongs to the same family as *Hoodia,* that is the Asclepiadaceae, is *Trichocaulon,* often with many-angled prickly stems, like long thick fingers, which usually lie flat on the ground. *Trichocaulon pedicellatum* has long, knobbly, finger-like leaves which grow downwards, whereas *T. clavatum* is small, roundish, upright and thornless.

Two species of Bushman's candle grow at the Skeleton Coast. *Sarcocaulon mossamedense,* with its distinctive pink flowers, sometimes light and sometimes dark, is most commonly seen. Less conspicuous is a small, dense prostrate variety which grows in isolated groups on gravel soil, and has been identified as *S. salmoniflorum.* It might well, however, be a new species as *S. salmoniflorum* is normally a dense shrub up to 1 m high. An interesting feature of the Bushman's candle is the dark brown, compact and resin-like bark of its tubular stem which helps retain moisture. As an additional measure to prevent unnecessary evaporation it sheds its leaves soon. The dried-out stems can be burned as incense and give off a pleasant aromatic smell.

Plants which look truly outlandish are the small stunted *Commiphora* trees with their thick, swollen stems, commonly called *kanniedood* (Afrikaans for 'cannot die'), which grow as squat, low-spreading shrubs. The rock commiphora, *Commiphora glaucescens,* is especially associated with coastal regions. It has smooth, golden-green bark and occurs as a shrub, but can grow as a tree of up to 4 m high. The oak-leaved commiphora, *C. wildii,* is endemic to Namibia and grows only in the northern Namib. It has a smooth, silvery grey-brown bark, stretched tightly over its relatively thick short trunk, which contrasts with the

33

34

black dolomitic rocks among which it often grows, clinging to them like a creeper. Most of the commiphora species produce aromatic resins. In biblical times the fragrant resinous substance, myrrh, used in medicine, as perfume and incense, and the medicinal resin 'Balm of Gilead', were extracted from Arabian commiphora species. For most of the year commiphoras have no leaves. When the leaves appear it is for a brief period only, during March and April, and only if it has rained. The leaves are bright green and the berries usually red. Commiphoras sometimes resemble miniature baobab trees and also look as if they are standing upside down with their roots in the air.

Another well-known and cosmopolitan family of which three species occur on the Skeleton Coast is the Euphorbiaceae. The cactus-like *Euphorbia virosa*, with its angled, upright and spiny stems, grows among the rocks, generally on mountain slopes. It has a shape very like a candelabra and grows up to 1,5 m tall. The fruits are smallish, of a rusty-brown colour. Black rhino are very partial to these plants, and consume the stems as well as the fruit. *Euphorbia damarana* is the well-known plains euphorbia, *melkbos* (milk-bush) or *wolfsmilch* (wolves' milk). These plants are well-branched with slender, herbaceous silver-grey stems, which are not spiny, and bear a yellow, fig-like fruit. The *Euphorbia giessii* is similar but smaller, with more laterally growing branchlets, which taper to a point. Typical of the euphorbias is their milky latex (hence the name 'milkbush', *melkbos*), which in some species is poisonous. If it comes in contact with the eyes, it can cause severe inflammation and even result in blindness.

One species of lithops or 'flowering stone' is found on the Skeleton Coast. *Lithops ruschiorum* has the rather descriptive name of Bushman's or Hottentot's buttocks and is also sometimes referred to as the Kaokoland lithops. The outstanding characteristic of these small succulents is their highly efficient camouflage: *L. ruschiorum* is a rusty pink and can hardly be distinguished from the pink feldspar gravels among which it grows. It bears a single yellow flower, which appears between the two cheeks of the 'buttocks' after it has rained in April and May. A fresh pair of leaves grows each year, almost as if a new plant emerges between the old 'buttocks', making it possible to calculate the age of the plant by counting the dried-out leaves lying next to it.

VEGETATION OF THE GRAVEL PLAINS

Several species of *Helichrysum*, generally known as everlastings or *sewejaartjies*, grow on the gravel plains, some in an upright position and others prostrate. A particularly striking one is the rounded bush-like *Helichrysum roseo-niveum*, called the desert edelweiss. The dense layer of silvery white hairs on the leaves gives the plant a soft gossamer appearance. The flowers vary from light to dark pink and have yellow centres. The plant as a whole looks more like a cultivated old-fashioned posy than a desert xerophyte growing under arid and harsh conditions.

One of the most intriguing forms of plant life in the desert is lichen, of which a wide variety occurs on the gravel plains, rocky outcrops and mountain slopes. Not likely to be noticed by the uninitiated, these strange organisms, which are normally hard and brittle, come to life or 'bloom' when water is sprinkled over them, moving visibly and becoming soft and leathery to the touch. Seen through a strong magnifying glass or close-up lens, an untidy-looking piece of rock turns into a shimmering segment of multi-coloured coral as the lichen absorbs the moisture.

Lichens are not really plants, but composite organisms composed of algae and fungi. This association is generally considered to be symbiotic, meaning that both the alga and the fungus derive benefit from the association. Because they 'help' one another they can grow in places where no other plant could exist. The alga furnishes food, which it builds up photosynthetically, to the fungus, while the fungus supplies moisture and shelter for the alga. The fungus is generally the larger component and determines the form which the plant takes. Lichens multiply by the distribution of small pieces of the plant body, or by germination of the fungal component. When free from the fungus the alga may exist normally, but the fungal component of the lichen cannot live separated from the alga. A crustose type of lichen grows on rocks and stones, sometimes several different species on the same stone, in colours ranging from yellow, blue, white, black, orange and red to different shades of green. Another form of lichen, which sometimes looks like small, fern-like bushes, generally orange or light green, grows on stones or dry wood. There are several species of wind-blown or wandering lichen, some resembling small round bushes, others rather like small, dried-up tubular leaves, generally black, turning green when watered. The latter variety tends to clump up in indentations, looking like dark mats of dry seaweed. Growing on stones and pebbles, lichen sometimes covers an entire plain and gives it an orange or green appearance.

A black 'barren' plain can be transformed into a lush green meadow overnight if the coastal fog has pushed inland to drench it. Like other desert vegetation, lichen is dependent on the fog for its survival, although it can manage without moisture for long periods of time.

Lichens which grow on rocks are slow but efficient 'soil formers': the rock is disintegrated gradually by their action and adds yearly to the increment of new soil. Lichen has an extremely slow reproductive cycle, and grows at most 1 mm per year.

The lichen communities of the Namib have created considerable interest among international lichen experts. Where it had originally been thought that there were not many more than a dozen kinds, recent researchers have already identified over a hundred different species. From a research and conservation point of view, the lichen fields of the gravel plains are the most threatened, as people drive their vehicles heedlessly over them, unaware of their intrinsic and interest value, and of how much damage they are doing. In dry areas lichens are ecologically important as they colonise habitats by influencing ground stability, hydrology, fertility and the microclimate. They are an important link in the food-chain of the desert and there is a close interaction between lichens and the insect life. Other than the enclosure of several lichen communities in the vicinity of Cape Cross, the lichens of the Namib are not protected.

The most unusual plant found in the Namib is the living fossil plant *Welwitschia mirabilis,* which grows at several locations on the Skeleton Coast. It has been termed a weird botanical wonder, the most baffling plant ever discovered and the most extraordinary curiosity of all living organisms. Welwitschias grow in a narrow belt between 30 and 40 km wide which runs parallel to the sea, about 30 to 40 km inland, from Swakopmund in the south more or less all the way up to Mossamedes in Angola. The best specimens grow among the hills of the Messum Crater. Here they are sheltered from the winds and do not have the forlorn and wind-shredded look of the welwitschias of the plains.

The welwitschia plant is actually a tree which has been dwarfed by the rigours of the desert climate. The largest specimens have stems which are up to 1,5 m in diameter, rising 2 m above the ground. Contrary to legend the fibrous

36

37

38

39

The living fossil plant, **Welwitschia mirabilis**, described by Charles Darwin as the platypus of the plant kingdom, was first recorded by Dr Friedrich Welwitsch after he had happened on a specimen in south-west Angola in 1859.

Previous page

38 Early morning fog, typical of the Skeleton Coast, is gradually dispersed by a pale desert sun.
39 A crazy paving of sun-baked mud slabs, formed from fine silt left behind by a recent flash flood, is flanked by bushes of **Sueda plumosa,** commonly referred to as brack-bush.

tap-root is relatively shallow, with many lateral roots just below the soil surface. The crown of the stem is flattened and saucer-shaped, dark-brown, hard and woody, almost resembling an inverted elephant's foot, protruding just above ground level as a rock-like hump.

The plant produces only two leaves throughout its lifetime, and if these two leaves die, the plant dies. They develop opposite each other and throughout the lifetime of the plant grow from the base outwards, up to 3 m long. The leaf-blades are tough and leathery but torn into long, thong-like shreds, constantly blackened and worn away by the desert sun and searing winds. The result is a great dishevelled mass of tangled leaves piled up on the desert surface like a discarded jumble of wool. Most surprising about the leaves is their very extensive leaf surface, unlike most xerophytes which have a reduced leaf surface in order to limit water loss through the stomata or pores. This is the clue to the welwitschia's survival: millions of stomata are distributed on both upper and lower leaf surfaces and these absorb fog moisture.

The welwitschia is dioecious, that is, the male and female flowers are on separate plants. The female plant produces up to one hundred of the cone-like flowers in one season. The male plant produces an abundance of pollen which is blown about by the dry autumn winds. The cones are often brightly coloured, the male cones salmon pink, the female ones greenish-yellow banded with reddish-brown and much larger.

It was originally thought that the conspicuous red beetle, *Probergrothius sexpunctatis*, was the welwitschia's pollinating agent. This insect, which changes from bright red to yellow with black spots as it matures, is found only in association with welwitschias and is also endemic to the Namib. It is especially common on the female plants, where it sucks sap from the young ones, destroying the developing seed. It has now been established, however, that pollination is caused by the winds. Only about one tenth of one per cent of welwitschia seed is finally available for germination, which even then will germinate only if fairly heavy rain falls over a period of several days. As this does not often happen, it explains why in some colonies the plants all appear to be more or less the same age.

Welwitschias are not only of ancient origin but are also very long-lived, most certainly among the oldest plants in the world. The age of one of the larger specimens has been estimated at a minimum of 2 000 years, while the age of average specimens has been estimated by carbon-14 dating as being between 500 and 600 years. Needless to say, these plants are protected and heavy penalties are incurred when people are caught removing or damaging them.

Overleaf

40　The photograph overleaf illustrates the disfigurement which is caused by prospecting for minerals. In high-rainfall areas sites such as these become washed over or overgrown within a relatively short period of time. In the desert, however, the scars are permanent. Contrary to popular belief, wind and sand do not gradually cover up the damage but rather tend to accentuate it.

41　Vegetation-topped dunes tend to occur in clusters, and particularly in the case of brack-bush hummocks often develop into large and humpy composite dunes.

40

41

The River Courses

... lifelines of the desert

T HE RIVERS WHICH drain across the northern Namib towards the sea are major components of the character and ecology of the Skeleton Coast. In prehistoric times when they were perennial and flowed wide and deep they played an important role in the formation of the desert landscape as it is today. They now bring plant forms from the interior that are normally foreign to a desert environment, which in turn attract a wide spectrum of animal life. This accounts for the biological variety, diverse habitat and multiformity of landscape which makes the Skeleton Coast one of the most extraordinary desert ecosystems in the world.

The apparently dry river courses have considerable quantities of subterranean water which sustain the comparatively rich vegetation. This in turn supports an infinite variety of insects, reptiles, larger and smaller mammals and birds. Transverse rock barriers force some of this water to the surface, thereby creating permanent and semi-permanent waterholes and the so-called 'gorras', waterholes under the surface, which are dug open by elephant and gemsbok. The river courses serve as natural 'pantries' for the springbok, gemsbok, ostrich and other resident animals of the mountains and plains. When food supplies elsewhere run low towards the end of the year, and especially in dry years, the animals move into the river courses and feed on the vegetation. Here the ana tree, *Acacia albida,* plays a major role. Unlike the other acacias, which flower from August to September, the ana tree flowers in May, June and July, shedding its highly nutritious pods in September, October and November, the driest time of the year when food is in short supply.

RIVERS THAT REACH THE SEA

A river that has become comparatively well known by virtue of the much-publicised 'desert' elephants which move up and down its course is the Hoanib. Although not the largest of the Skeleton Coast rivers, the Hoanib with its extensive flood-plain sustains the largest animal populations in the northern Namib. It originates in the Joubert Mountains and passes through the Khowareb Schlucht and Sesfontein on its way to the coast. The salt-pans that occur in its wake once it has passed through the dunes are caused by evaporation; several of these are surrounded by reed growth and sustain small numbers of game.

Overleaf

42 The narra bush, **Acanthosicyos horrida,** grows in the desert under extreme conditions. Instead of leaves it has long green paired thorns on its stem, through which it photosynthesises. The prickly fruit is eaten by gemsbok, hyaena and porcupine, as well as by the Himba people, who regard it as a delicacy.

43 These shrub-coppice dunes are often referred to as 'zebra dunes'. In the same way that each zebra has its own individual pattern of stripes, each dune has its own original arrangement of magnetite ridges and rivulets.

Sand continually fills up the river-beds, to be washed away to the sea when the river comes down in flood.

The Hoanib reaches the sea only on very rare occasions, such as in 1982, when the exceptional rains in northern Kaokoland and Damaraland caused all the rivers in the northern Namib to break through to the sea, in the case of the Hoanib for the first time in nineteen years. Normally it is stopped by the wide belt of transverse dunes which runs parallel to the coastline from Torra Bay towards the Kunene, which has resulted in the development of the extensive

42

43 ▷

flood-plain, the rich deposits of alluvial silt fertilising the prolific growth of vegetation which sustains the animal life. The vegetation consists of a variety of reeds and grasses, tamarisk (*Tamarix usneoides*), wild fig (*Ficus sycomorus*), mustard tree (*Salvadora persica*), ebony tree (*Euclea pseudebenus*) and several species of acacia, such as *Acacia tortilis* and *Acacia albida* and further inland *Acacia erioloba*. Apart from elephant, other large animals which occur in the Hoanib River course are giraffe, gemsbok, springbok and baboon, and occasionally lion.

The Hoanib is also of certain historical interest. The Thirstland Trekkers from Angola ventured down as far as its northern banks to hunt elephant. Dates ranging from 1900 to 1910 and names chiselled out on stones in the Khowareb Schlucht bear witness to these illegal hunting trips. Captain Smith, who led the expedition which rescued the castaways of the Dunedin Star in 1942, drove his convoy along the Hoanib river-bed, in the course of which his vehicles became endlessly bogged down in the thick sand.

Possibly the most versatile of the rivers of the Skeleton Coast is the Hoarusib. It is the largest west-flowing river between the Kunene and the Orange Rivers and reaches the sea regularly every year, often more than once. It has its source in Kaokoland in the vicinity of Opuwa and flows down through the Tonnesen and Giraffe Mountains. At Purros, where it is joined by the Gomatum, it enters a narrow canyon and, making for unusual and spectacular scenery, twists and turns down to the sea. It probably derives its name from this last stretch. The Nama word *!naruseb* means water which twists and turns through a narrow gorge. The perennial spring at Purros has meant survival for many of the local

The 'white castles' of the Hoarusib Canyon spread into the gorges and rock crevices, presiding like a Buddha or the sphinx over the river-bed below.

inhabitants, who lost their cattle during the 1980 drought and who have since managed to eke out an existence by cultivating mealies and pumpkins.

The features of the Hoarusib River are many and varied. Especially characteristic are the steep canyon walls of black and red volcanic rock, the makalani palms which have grown from pips washed down from the north-east, and the monumental white 'castles' or 'temples', formations of yellowish-white sedimentary clay, the origin of which dates back to prehistoric times. There are similar deposits in rivers further south, which suggests an era of low rainfall followed by one of high rainfall in times long past. Also typical of the Hoarusib are the elephants which move up and down its length, although during the late 1970s they dwindled from a resident herd of seventeen to a single bull and three young cows.* There is plenty of water along the river course and periodically game such as springbok, gemsbok, jackal and even zebra work their way up and down the canyon. In the upper reaches lappet-faced vultures nest on the tops of the taller trees.

The Khumib is a wide, expansive river which rises in the mountains around Sanitatas and Orupembe. Although not a particularly large river, it has considerable quantities of underground water with which it sustains the mopane, *Colophospermum mopane*, and leadwood, *Combretum imberbe*, trees which grow along its course. The local name for the latter, *omumborumbonga*, is acoustically descriptive of its spectacularly long, gnarled and intertwined roots, sometimes up to 50 m in length, which have become exposed by floodwaters. The Khumib does not come down every year. The old Khumib delta, which dates back to a time when the level of the sea was considerably higher than it is today, has steep sides which are gradually being eaten away by the tide. On misty days these cliffs of sand which cascade endlessly onto the beach make for intriguing scenery, as enigmatic and impenetrable as the image which is created by the name 'Skeleton Coast'.

The Khumib has several springs, the best known of which is Sarusas Fountain, a strong and permanent source of water, even in the worst of droughts. The vegetation is colourful, especially typical being the narra plant, *Acanthosicyos horrida*. These light green straggly bushes grow in association with dunes, spreading their spiny branches over the sides to resemble uneven and prickly umbrellas. Narra bushes have a round spiny fruit with a high moisture and protein content to which porcupines and springbok are especially partial. On several occasions hyaena, of all animals, have been observed feeding off narra fruit. Animals seen in the Khumib River course are mainly gemsbok, springbok and ostrich, and further inland giraffe and rhino, occasionally even elephant. From time to time lion and cheetah venture down as far as Sarusas Fountain to drink.

Few people are aware of the fact that there is a Koichab River in the northern as well as in the southern Namib, the latter being the river from which Lüderitz draws its water. The name 'Koichab', a Nama word which means brack or very salty bush, is descriptive of the humpy fields of brack-bush dunes through which the northern Koichab passes before it reaches the sea east of Torra Bay. Springbokwater, where Nature Conservation has its control post for entry into the Skeleton Coast Park from the interior, lies in the Koichab's course and has a spring with extremely brack water, which also bears out the river's name.

The popular Terrace Bay angling resort draws its water from the Unjab or Uniab, another river which in times gone by must have been very large, emptying its water into an extensive delta. West of the dune belt the Uniab reaches the sea along several courses, all of which cross this delta. A similar series of high sand cliffs occur along the beach as in the case of the Khumib further north. There are

Overleaf

44   A patterned curtain of sand threatens to envelop the evergreen bulrushes of a desert river-bed.

45   With the exception of the Orange River on the southern and the Kunene River on the northern borders, the Hoarusib is the only river in Namibia that flows into the sea every year. Here it winds its way down the Hoarusib Canyon through steep walls of sand and rock.

* Calves were subsequently born to this group.

83

Reminiscent of an ancient ruin, this wall of mud and sand deposited by the Khumib River is rapidly being eroded by the wind.

many reed-encircled waterholes in the old delta which sustain resident populations of springbok and gemsbok, as well as an interesting variety of birds such as flamingoes, cormorants, teals and moorhens. An interesting feature of the Uniab is the unexpected and refreshing waterfall not far from its mouth. Dwindling numbers of elephant, rhino and lion occur in the upper reaches,* which lie among the flat, brick-red, Karoo-like Etendeka formations in the north-west of Damaraland.

The Huab is a colourful river which passes through the vivid yellow sediments, brick-red and grey lava koppies and plains west of Twyfelfontein, and winds down through a graphic landscape of black basaltic extrusions as it approaches the sea. Long stretches of dry river-bed are interspersed with green reed-encircled pools which support mostly gemsbok. The only bridge in the Skeleton Coast was built over the Huab by Ben du Preez in the sixties when he was actively prospecting for diamonds at Terrace Bay and Toscanini. Named after his partner Jack Scott, the bridge is a narrow and precarious-looking structure which is seldom used, although it justified its existence in 1982 when the road to Terrace Bay at the Huab turned into an impassable quagmire from the drenching rains. The remains of an oil drill, also erected by the intrepid Ben du Preez, can still be seen at the mouth of the Huab. Du Preez never found oil but it was rumoured that he had found rich deposits of anthracite, which were, however, too deep to mine economically at the time.

* As a result of increased control, game numbers are gradually increasing in these areas.

The Ugab River has the distinction of being the southern boundary of the Skeleton Coast Park, with the Nature Conservation control post for visitors to the area situated on its southern bank about 15 km from its mouth. It has its source in the vicinity of Outjo and flows through the extensive Ugab Valley, with its eroded landscape of flat-topped Ugab terraces, past the Vingerklip, an erosional monolith of limestone conglomerate and a well-known Namibian landmark. Once in the Namib the Ugab meanders through an expansive range of mica schist ridges, compressed, folded and lying on their sides, and reaches the sea approximately 60 km north of Cape Cross. It comes down in flood fairly regularly and reaches the sea every one or two years. It has typical riverine vegetation in the form of ana trees (*Acacia albida*), tamarisk (*Tamarix usneoides*), and wild fig (*Ficus sycomorus*), which are sustained by its considerable supplies of underground water. Its series of reed-encircled waterholes are frequented mainly by springbok. Of the relatively large numbers of black rhino which used to gather in its lower reaches, very few remain. That there was a great deal of game at one time is evidenced by the relief rock carvings of rhino, giraffe and other animals on the river banks.

RIVERS THAT END IN SAND

Contrary to most maps the Sechomib does not reach the sea, but peters out into a large dry mud-pan. Until 1982 when, as the result of a cloudburst, it came down with a vengeance it had not reached this pan in at least a hundred years. It divided into as many as eleven different courses and turned the pan into a damp and sticky quagmire. In the process it transformed one of its better-known springs, formerly a series of tranquil ponds surrounded by grass and quicksand against a backdrop of striking lava hillocks, into a gaping canyon, with steep ravine-like sides and a small but steep waterfall, rather similar to the Sesriem Canyon in the south of Namibia. Interesting and ancient mud sediments were washed open and shells which date back to a warm-water era became exposed.

Although prominently featured on Automobile Association and South African Airways maps as of equal size and importance as the Kunene, Hoarusib and Swakop Rivers, the Nadas, sometimes spelt Natas, is a minor and rather nondescript river which peters out into the salt-pans at Cape Frio. What makes it interesting, however, is that when one looks at aerial photographs it becomes clear that in prehistoric times the Nadas must have been a huge river, while the present-day Cape Frio salt-pans must formerly have been part of its original delta. Its other distinction is the Nadas Spring, situated in its upper reaches, close to its source in Kaokoland, which is frequented by game and the local inhabitants.

The Munutum River's interesting features are the Okau Spring, an attractive reed-encircled waterhole set among honeycomb-patterned volcanic rock formations, and the fantastically-shaped granite outcrops, or 'petrified ghosts' of the Skeleton Coast. Normally an extremely dry river, it also came down strongly in 1982, ripping open a hitherto unknown arm and exposing a deep chasm, giving, as it is already filling up with sand, only a brief glimpse into the hidden highways and byways of its former tributaries.

Winding its way through the Hartmann and Otjihipa Mountains of Kaokoland, banked by white lime cliffs and a luxuriant growth of mopane, the Odondojengo is as attractive as its name. It disappears into the aptly named Engo Valley, a spectacular and almost surreal expanse of salmon-pink feldspar wastes which gradually runs into a sea of narra-topped dunes. The desert lizard,

Overleaf

46 The Khumib River carves its way to the sea through the mud deposits of its ancient delta, which was formed in primeval times when the river was much larger and the sea level considerably higher than it is today.

46

47

48

Angolosaurus skoogi, named after a Captain Skoog who found the first known specimen in Angola in 1912, occurs in the vegetationless dunes of the Engo Valley. Like the *Aporosaura* lizard, it does a weird syncopated, alternate front and back foot-lifting dance to keep its body temperature down as it basks on the slipface of a dune, diving into the loose sand with a screwing movement at the slightest provocation.

THE ONLY PERENNIAL RIVER

To this day the Kunene River, destination of many of the earlier explorers, has retained a romantic aura of adventure and discovery. It forms the boundary between the Skeleton Coast and Angola, and at the same time is the north-western border of Namibia. The confluence of several rivers which rise deep in the highlands of Angola, banked on either side by towering mountain ranges, it becomes Namibia's fastest-flowing river as it descends rapidly towards the sea, plummeting through narrow gorges and ravines, generating vast resources of potential energy. Engineers maintain that another fourteen hydro-electric power stations such as the Ruacana plant could be built on the Kunene, which would enable Namibia to export large supplies of hydro-electricity to neighbouring countries.

The river was named by Herero migrating from central Africa in a south-westerly direction. When they entered the Kaokoveld the river was on their right, and they called it *okunene*, meaning the large or right arm; to the Herero the right arm is the larger of the two. The land on their left they called *okaoko*, meaning land to the left, that is, south of the Kunene, from where the name Kaokoveld, which later became Kaokoland, was derived. In ancient times the Kunene was an inland river which emptied its contents into the Etosha Pan, much as the Okavango River drains into the Okavango Swamps today. The Oshana Otaka appears to have been the arterial limb along which the Kunene's water flowed into the Etosha Basin in the west of the Etosha Plain, and this must have been the lower course of the Kunene before erosion diverted the main channel westward to empty out in the Atlantic Ocean. From time to time flood-waters still find their way into the pan at Etaka.

In former years vast numbers of elephant, rhino, black-faced impala, hippo and crocodile frequented the banks and waters of the Kunene, but these have largely been exterminated. Other than migrating elephants and considerable numbers of crocodiles very little remains of what must once have been a hunter's paradise. Willem van der Riet, the first person to navigate the Kunene in a canoe, maintained that the Kunene crocodiles were by far the most fearsome and aggressive he had ever come across.

The aquatic life of the Kunene, and particularly of its mouth, holds much of interest, especially for the researcher. Huge leather-backed turtles, up to 1 m and more in length, teem in the estuary, while considerable populations of common water turtles occur higher up in the river. Marine fauna not normally associated with cold-water conditions occur in the Kunene mouth, such as 'springers', a kind of herring, leather fish or 'leer' fish, which in angling terms are as challenging to catch as tiger fish, and, about 1 km from the mouth and further inland, freshwater shrimps. These are quite large, up to 10 cm long, and are caught in nets, mainly off the Angolan shore. By all accounts they are quite delicious — hardly fare one would expect to find in a harsh desert environment.

Because they add contrast to the desert's colours, and contour to its shape,

Previous page

47   Against a backdrop of cascading sand, lappet-faced vultures **Torgos tracheliotus**, nest on the top of an ana tree, **Acacia albida**, in the Hoarusib Canyon. These vultures are extremely sensitive to human disturbance. In the Namib-Naukluft Park further south their breeding rate has declined alarmingly as a result of mining and tourist activities.

48   The white 'temples' or 'castles' of the Hoarusib, formations of yellowish-white sedimentary clay, date back to prehistoric times and are remnants of ancient river silt deposits. Some of these formations are up to 40 m high.

it is above all the visual impact that these rivers have on visitors which makes them such an integral part of the desert experience. The unexpected ribbon of brilliant green among the subtle and muted desert shades makes an indelible impression, as does a group of springbok drinking at a waterhole surrounded by a sea of towering sand-dunes. The rains of 1982 demonstrated the inexorable and self-renewing forces with which the rivers continuously change and reshape the desert profile, ever generating something new into the primeval landscape of the Skeleton Coast.

Overleaf
49   Ostriches meander across the barren pastel wastes of the Engo Valley.

50   Granitic gneiss is patterned by a combination of wind erosion and fog action.

51   The weird hedgehog-like **Adenia pechuelii**, commonly known as elephant's foot, often roots in rock crevices, firmly anchored by its taproot. The genus **Adenia** is a member of the **Granadilla** or passion-fruit family, Passifloraceae.

49

50

51

The Fauna

...adapted to a desert habitat

BECAUSE PEOPLE DO not expect to see animals in a desert environment, the sight of a solitary elephant walking over a sand-dune has a far greater impact than that of a large herd trumpeting around a waterhole in a game reserve. To the uninitiated the wealth of fauna which occurs at the Skeleton Coast comes as a revelation. Other than the more obvious animals such as the elephant, rhino and lion of the river courses and the springbok, ostrich and gemsbok of the plains, the apparently barren dunes harbour a specialised fauna that is unique in the world. Utilising windblown detritus from the interior as a source of food and fog from the ocean as a source of moisture, a remarkable community of interdependent dune-dwelling insects, reptiles and small mammals has evolved, with specialised adaptations to ensure their survival. Adaptations such as thermoregulation, coloration, breeding strategies and nomadism have also ensured the survival of a surprising variety of desert birds. The birds of the coast find their sustenance in the rich plankton and pelagic resources of the Benguela Current, while the beaches are kept clean by ghost crabs, jackal and hyaena.

FAUNA OF THE RIVER COURSES

The animals that live in the dry river-beds of the desert are not necessarily typical desert fauna, in that they have regular access to water and feed on vegetation which also occurs in the interior. The larger species such as elephant, lion and

Previous page
52 The Himbas, of Herero origin, eke out a marginal existence in the peripheral areas of the desert. Their staple diet consists of goat's milk and meat and to some extent veldkos. In some areas their goats cause extensive damage to the habitat.

rhino are migratory, and move up and down the river courses, often increasing in numbers when food becomes scarce in the interior.

The elephant, *Loxodonta africana*, of the Skeleton Coast decreased considerably in numbers after the implementation of the Odendaal proposals. (See the chapter, Political History and Development.) The eastern and western populations became separated, the former, because farms and homelands surrounding the park have cut off natural migration routes, converging in Etosha, where their numbers have increased to such an extent that it has become necessary to cull them. The western population, which is now more or less confined to western Damaraland and the lower reaches of the Skeleton Coast rivers has, on the other hand, decreased in numbers as a result of inadequate protection and consequent poaching and trophy hunting, compounded by the extreme drought conditions of the early eighties, and is now considered to be endangered. As a result of wide press coverage these 'desert' elephants have acquired an aura of romanticism and mystique. It has been suggested that they have special adaptations such as longer legs, large flat and spongy feet, that they can go without water for long periods of time and that they therefore belong to a separate species. This assumption is, however, not based on fact. The Hoanib elephants, other than being behaviourally adapted and special by virtue of the area that they inhabit, are physiologically no different to the elephants which occur in the Etosha National Park, or in the rest of Africa. To survive in the desert they have a wide range and will travel for distances of up to 60 km in a day along regular elephant paths over rugged terrain between the different springs. They also dig holes in the dry beds of the river courses, into which water seeps from below, at the same time providing a source of water for the other animals of the desert. The water is sometimes too deep for the baby elephants to reach, however, in which case the parent will draw it up in its trunk and deposit it into the youngster's mouth. They feed mainly on the vegetation in the river courses, such as mopane leaves, tamarisk, reeds and rushes, as well as the nutritious pods, bark and leaves of the ana tree.

Black rhino, *Diceros bicornis*, were at one time plentiful in both Damaraland and Kaokoland, and frequently moved into the Skeleton Coast down the river courses. As a result of uncontrolled poaching, however, they have become extremely scarce, and other than the occasional track are seldom seen at the Skeleton Coast. An estimated 45 still inhabit the southern regions of the adjacent Damaraland.* They are solitary animals, and wander within a wide home range as far as 100 to 150 km along regular paths which link up with waterholes, as they need to drink every second day. They feed on the twigs, leaves and bark of acacias, euphorbias and other bushes and trees, usually in the early mornings and at dusk, spending the greater part of the day sleeping in the shade of a tree or bush.

During the sixties Bernabé de la Bat, then Director of the Department of Nature Conservation and Tourism, became greatly concerned about the continued survival of black rhino in South West Africa. At that stage the entire population consisted of 90 animals, all of which were in the north-western part of the country, in an area where the Department had no jurisdiction and where poaching was rife. A capture and relocation programme was launched, in the process of which 76 black rhino were caught in Kaokoland and transported to the Etosha National Park. Today there is a viable population of over 300 animals in the park.

Lion, *Panthera leo*, appear and disappear in the river courses as the game on which they prey comes and goes, depending on grazing conditions in the interior.

Overleaf
53 Floodwaters level out as they reach the sea at the expansive mouth of the Hoarusib River.

54 The remains of the **Benguela Eagle**, wrecked 25 km north of the Ugab River mouth.

* These numbers have increased gradually, and there are now an estimated 60–70 rhino in this area.

95

53

54

55

56

Previous page

55 The placid sea belies the treacherousness of the coast, which has become the graveyard of countless ships and men.

56 One of the better-preserved wrecks is that of the **Montrose**. High and dry on the beach, it has become a popular rendezvous for cormorants and other seabirds. The many wrecks are caused by strong winds, frequent fogs and the cold Benguela Current which flows up from the South Pole, at times reaching speeds of between three and four knots.

They feed mainly on the gemsbok and springbok of the plains, by lying in wait for them at waterholes, and this is where the lions of the desert are usually encountered. After the unusually good rains in Kaokoland in 1982 the gemsbok and springbok of the plains moved inland and virtually overnight the lions at the coast found themselves with very little to eat, to the extent that they resorted to feeding off seals which they found on the beaches. They take the seals by surprise as they lie sleeping, kill them and then drag them to a sheltered place, sometimes for several kilometres when there are young to be fed. This unusual behaviour has not been recorded before, which makes it all the more interesting.

Giraffe, *Giraffa camelopardalis,* are often seen in the river courses and in latter years parties of chacma baboons, *Papio ursinus,* have been observed. Smaller animals which occur commonly are Cape hare, *Lepus capensis,* a small hare not unlike a rabbit in some of its features, the crested porcupine, *Hystrix africaeaustralis,* genet (small-spotted, *Genetta servalina*), caracal, *Felis caracal,* and African wild cat, *Felis lybica.*

An impressive bird occasionally seen in some of the river courses is the lappet-faced vulture, *Torgos tracheliotus,* which nests on the top of large acacia trees. They are large birds, with a wing-span of up to 2,5 m or more. These vultures are rare, although they have a wide distribution over the African continent. They are extremely vulnerable during their long breeding cycles, and build their nests away from communities of other species. They are easily disturbed by mining and tourist activities, as has been borne out by the decreased breeding rate of the lappet-faced vultures of the Namib-Naukluft Park. Because these birds breed only twice in three years, sometimes three times in four years, the species presents a considerable conservation problem.

The tree-lined river courses harbour a wide variety of smaller birds, such as Cape sparrows, *Passer melanurus,* mountain chats, *Oenanthe monticola,* and bokmakieries, *Telophorus zeylonus,* characterised by their melodious calls, as well as titbabblers, *Parisoma subcaerulum,* redeyed bulbuls, *Pycnonotus nigricans* and mousebirds, *Colius* spp. Several species of birds are found at the waterholes, of which the most commonly seen are Egyptian geese, *Alopochen aegyptiacus,* avocets, *Recurvirostra avosetta,* red-knobbed coots, *Fulica cristata,* and Cape teals, *Anas capensis.*

FAUNA OF THE DUNES

No other sand-dune system in the world has an animal life comparable to that of the sand-dunes of the Namib. An established pattern of food and water chains revolves around the all-important fog moisture generated by the Benguela Current and the detritus consisting of animal and plant material which is blown into the dunes. This organic matter on which the dune creatures feed is blown in from the hinterland, or from the plains and corridors between the dunes where grass springs up after the occasional rain shower, and is stored indefinitely as a food supply for the many primary dune-dwellers such as termites, beetles, fish moths and ants which are preyed on by lizards, snakes, spiders, crickets, flies, scorpions, chameleons and wasps.

Most picturesque and relatively well known is the colourful translucent gecko, *Palmatogecko rangei.* It can run at considerable speeds, holding itself high above the surface of the ground, leaving fig-like imprints with its specialised webbed feet and diving into the loose sand at great speed, disappearing in a second. With its thin, virtually transparent skin, the *Palmatogecko* is almost ethereal in appearance. Its body is a delicate salmon pink, with white markings along the belly and on the feet, and the eyes are large, dark and protruding with white lids and turquoise blue spots directly behind them on the head. It is exclusively nocturnal, feeds on smaller insects and is preyed on by the dancing white lady spider, hunting spiders and the sidewinder adder. Two lizards commonly found in the dunes of the Skeleton Coast are the large yellow and orange vegetarian lizard, *Angolosaurus skoogi*, of which the male has a shiny black chin and throat, and the shovel-nosed lizard, *Aporosaura anchietae.* These lizards dive beneath the sand with a rapid corkscrewing movement when disturbed, and perform a thermoregulatory footlifting dance, holding the tail high up above the sand to keep cool. Legless lizards are occasionally seen, but very briefly, as they are strictly nocturnal.

Unique to the Namib are the unusually coloured 'white' *Onymacris* Tenebrionid beetles, of which the white *O. bicolor*, the white and yellow *O. langi* and the yellow *O. marginipennis* occur in the Skeleton Coast dunes. Researchers have found that the abdominal white or yellow topside or elytra of these beetles, which covers most of their upper surface, reduces their body temperatures by up to 5° C, which means that they are able to remain active on the dune surface after their black relatives have had to dive into the sand to avoid overheating. In cooler zones, such as the northern Namib, they are able to operate in the heat of the day, and are thus ideally suited for optimum existence in the Skeleton Coast. Of the same genus and also seen at the Skeleton Coast is the shiny black, long-legged *O. unguicularis.* This beetle, which has been termed a 'living condensation unit', is active during the warmer parts of the day. On mornings when fog has penetrated the dune area and enveloped the dune slipfaces where they lie buried for the night, they surface and make their way to the crest of the dune. Here, turning towards the wind, they let the fog condense on their bodies. They then lift themselves up by their back legs into a headstanding position so that the drops run forward towards their mouths and they can drink their fill.

Snakes found amongst the dunes are the sidewinding adder, *Bitis peringueyi*, which drinks by sucking droplets of condensed moisture from its body, and a type of horned adder, *B. caudalis.* These two snakes give bites that are painful but not dangerous. The sidewinder takes refuge in the sand during the daytime, lying with only the eyes, which are situated conveniently on top of its head, showing above the surface. Its eyes and skin closely resemble the quartz sand grains and are therefore an excellent camouflage. The sidewinder's tracks, a diagonal series of broken transverse lines, are very distinctive.

A conspicuous spider which occurs in the dunes is the lady trapdoor spider, *Leucorchestris* sp., also called the dancing white lady. This spider constructs its home by digging a hole in the sand and covering the walls with a cobweb lining to prevent the loose sand from filling it in. A kind of trapdoor, which is closed when the spider is inside, is constructed over the hole. Black dune wasps prey on these spiders. Paralysing the spider with its sting, the wasp places it in a burrow in the sand and lays an egg on its body. The larval wasp eventually feeds on the living body of the spider. The trapdoor spider has a peculiar escape mechanism when threatened: in an attempt to evade its predators, it will form itself into a tight ball and roll rapidly down a dune slope.

FAUNA OF THE PLAINS

Larger mammals seen most commonly on the plains are springbok and gemsbok.

Overleaf

57 Dwarfed by its environment this lone 'desert' elephant patrols the lower reaches of the Hoarusib River.

58 The sphinx-like clay sediments and makalani palms, **Hyphaene ventricosa,** give Leylandt's Drift in the Hoarusib Canyon an ambience of ancient Egypt.

59 The prevailing south-west wind sweeps a continuous saraband of sand from dune to dune. The two dunes in the foreground are typical barchans.

57

58

59

In years when in desert terms good rain-showers occur and there is sufficient grass cover, their numbers increase and even zebra will move in from the interior, followed by beasts of prey such as hyaena, lion and leopard. Springbok, *Antidorcas marsupialis*, are ideally suited to desert conditions, as they are opportunistic feeders which will both browse and graze, depending on what is available. When the grass supply has become depleted they feed on the nutritious brack-bush. They are able to go without water for considerable lengths of time, but will drink regularly when it is available. At the Skeleton Coast they are usually seen in small groups, although when it is very dry in the interior larger herds move into the desert areas.

Where springbok appear particularly graceful and elegant in the harsh desert environment, the much larger, geometrically patterned gemsbok, *Oryx gazella*, is especially striking. It is also well suited to desert conditions as its diet of grasses, wild melons, the fruit of the narra plant, bulbs of succulents and even welwitschia leaves enables it to go without water for long periods of time. Like the camel, the gemsbok has an unusual adaptation in the form of a built-in radiator system in its nasal passages, which cools the blood on its way to its brain and reduces the need to perspire.

There is a surprising variety of birds on the open plains. Larks are very common, of which the diminutive Gray's lark, *Ammomanes grayi*, is very much in evidence on the plains within the fog belt, where it feeds on seeds and insects. It is small and pale in colour, builds open cap-shaped nests in which it lays its eggs and is the only truly endemic Namib bird. One of the most interesting groups of birds is the sandgrouse, which because of specific adaptations is restricted to arid areas. The Namaqua sandgrouse, *Pterocles namaqua*, occurs most commonly on the gravel plains. These birds feed almost exclusively on small dry seeds and it is therefore necessary for them to drink regularly. About two hours after sunrise they gather at waterholes in large flocks until there are hundreds, sometimes thousands at a time. They drink with great caution, flying off noisily immediately after taking a few sips. Breeding sandgrouse make no nests, they simply lay their eggs in shallow scrapes in the ground, where their buff-coloured spotted plumage keeps them well camouflaged from predators. The females incubate during the day and to combat temperatures of up to 50° C they raise their body feathers to increase the insulating layer of air immediately surrounding them, resorting to panting only when temperatures are extremely high. The newly-hatched chicks have to be provided with drinking water every day, which is brought to them by the male sandgrouse. With his uniquely modified breast feathers he absorbs water by wading into the shallows at waterholes, and carries it back and exudes it in droplets for the chicks to drink.

Larger birds often seen on the plains are Ludwig's bustard, *Neotis ludwigii*, Rüppell's korhaan, *Eupodotis rueppellii*, and ostrich, *Struthio camelus*. The latter are very typical of the Skeleton Coast and are sometimes seen in large groups of up to fifty and more, although more commonly in small groups of two or three. Also a very typical bird, seen not only on the gravel plains but among the dunes, in the river courses and on the beaches, is the ubiquitous pied crow, *Corvus albus*, also referred to as the parson's crow. These birds cause a considerable amount of pollution, in that they carry refuse away from rubbish dumps or where it has been dug out by jackals, and distribute it all over the desert. The smaller black crow, *Corvus capensis*, is also seen, but generally more towards the interior.

Two species of whip snake, *Psammophis trigrammus*, called the western sand snake, and *P. leightoni namibensis*, the Namib sand snake, occur on the plains. They are long, slender and attractive snakes, rather shy and extremely fast moving. Their poison is not dangerous to humans. They feed primarily on small lizards, and possibly on the red and yellow beetles, *Probergrothius sexpunctatis*, which live in association with welwitschia plants.

The desert plains as well as the dunes and river-beds teem with several species of mice and gerbils, especially after a 'good' rain year. They are mainly nocturnal, very gregarious, to a large extent vegetarian and seemingly independent

Cape fox, **Vulpes chama**, are strictly nocturnal and very rarely seen. This one, Rommel, whose love for custard overcame his natural shyness, regularly visited the Sarusas mining camp.

of water. Another nocturnal animal, seldom seen, but very much present is the Cape fox, *Vulpes chama*, which feeds on insects and small mammals, birds and vegetable matter. A glimpse of this 'desert' fox is very rewarding as it has a quick, phantom-like grace when it flits in and out of the dark shadows with its long, dense bushy tail floating behind it like a silver cloud.

FAUNA OF THE BEACHES

Black-backed jackal, *Canis mesomelas*, which patrol up and down the beaches keeping them clean of dead seals, birds and fish, are a familiar sight at the Skeleton Coast. They are attractive and colourful animals with their bright rufous coats and the broad conspicuous dark mantle down their backs. In competition for the refuse and carrion cast up by the tides are brown hyaena, *Hyaena brunnea*, also self-appointed health officials of the coast. This shaggy dark brown animal with the thick mane along its back is seldom seen, however, as it is strictly nocturnal, but it makes its presence known by the resonant 'wah-wah-wah' of its distinctive call. Other scavengers of the coast are the ghost crabs, *Ocypode africana* and *O. cursor*, fair-weather creatures which live under the surface along the beaches, emerging when the sand is warmed up by the sun, and at the slightest provocation scuttling frenetically towards the sea, sometimes in large squadrons.

In contrast to the 'barrenness' of the desert is the immense richness of the

Overleaf
60   The Auses waterhole on the western side of the Hoanib flood-plain is a favourite haunt of the much-publicised, desert-adapted elephants.

adjacent ocean. The Benguela Current flows up from Antarctica laden with oxygen and a rich variety of zoo- and phytoplankton. This plankton is driven close to the shore by the west winds where the upwelling of the Benguela Current causes it to rise to the surface. Exposed to the energy of the sun, a plankton 'bloom' is produced which feeds large schools of pilchards and anchovies, on which seals, cormorants, gannets and many other marine creatures feed. The Namibian west coast at one time had one of the richest pelagic resources in the world, but because of the over-granting of fishing concessions in the early sixties and resultant over-utilisation of the resources, in addition to the large numbers

Battered by wind, sea and sand the steering cabin of the **Montrose** is a popular cormorants' perch.

— between 120 and 180 at any one time — of Russian, Polish, Japanese and other trawlers which fish further out, the profitability of the fishing industries of Walvis Bay and Lüderitz has been seriously impaired. Fish quotas have been drastically cut, and there are signs of a gradual recovery, but it will take many years before resources build up to the level of former years. The west coast is still, nevertheless, an anglers' paradise, the most popular fish being galjoen, steenbras, kabeljou and kolstert.

The most numerous of the coastal birds are Cape cormorants, *Phalacrocorax capensis*. They are also the main producers of guano, an estimated one million birds inhabiting the guano platforms along the coast. Cormorants need up to 15 per cent of their body weight in food per day, and when they breed up to 20 per cent. To gain the best use of the rich pelagic resources they synchronise their

An island of seemingly irresolute ostrich in an expansive waste of sand and rocks.

Two species of ghost crab, **Ocypode africana** and **O. cursor**, occur along the beaches of the Skeleton Coast.

61

62

61 The rusting machinery of innumerable abandoned mining attempts, disintegrating oil rigs, corroding drills and abject heaps of indescribable rubbish not only bear witness to some of the biggest fiascos in Namibia's mining history, but have defaced the desert landscape permanently.

62 The large vegetarian lizard, **Angolosaurus skoogi**, which is endemic to the northern Namib. It was named after a certain Captain Skoog who found a single specimen in 1912 in southern Angola. It was, however, formally identified and named only about 50 years later. As the photograph was taken, a second lizard (on the left) dived and disappeared into the sand at lightning speed.

63 The hull of the **Suiderkus**. Some of the wreckage found on the coast dates back 400 years, when ships of the Dutch East India Company and Portuguese seafarers sailed around the Cape en route to India.

breeding with the wind regimes which provide the conditions for the rich plankton soup on which pilchards and anchovies feed. Small flocks of Damara terns, *Sterna balaenarum*, are a common sight along the Skeleton Coast. This bird, considered to be an endangered species, is endemic and restricted to the west coast of Southern Africa. Damara terns lay their eggs about one kilometre inland on the open gravel plains in small holes scooped in the sand, in the same way as seagulls. Several species of gulls are found along the coast, and at coastal lagoons and waterholes lesser and greater flamingoes, *Phoenicopterus minor* and *P. ruber*.

There are two seal colonies along the Skeleton Coast. The larger of these is at Cape Cross and has become a popular tourist attraction, while the smaller is at Cape Frio further north. The seals of these colonies are Cape fur seals, *Arctocephalus pusillus*, the largest of the world's nine fur seal species, which breeds only on the west coast of Southern Africa. The Cape Cross fur seals are culled on a regular basis. An interesting adaptation of these seals is how, as warm-blooded creatures, they keep warm in the cold water of the Benguela Current. This is achieved by two layers of hair and a layer of blubber beneath the skin. The outer hairs act as a waterproof coating, underneath which the inner layer of fine hairs remains dry. Air trapped in this system, however, causes a heat-stress problem when the seals come ashore and when they bask on the rocks in the sun. Physiological adaptations, such as the lighter covering of hair on their flippers and the fact that their extremities are bare and have large sweat glands, allow excess heat to be dissipated through convection and evaporation. This is why seals are often seen lying with their flippers held erect in the breeze, which maximises this cooling effect. The bulls often use their hind flippers to scrape away the layer of warm surface sand to reach the cooler sand underneath.

Whales were once plentiful in the seas off the Namib coast, but by the turn of the century the large, mostly American, whaling fleets had ensured that none remained. The only evidence that they were once there in large numbers is their bleached bones lying forsaken on the beaches. Hopefully, the conservation measures practised at present will prevent a similar fate befalling the other creatures of the Skeleton Coast.

Early Explorers

. . . lured by the unknown

64 The desert-adapted gemsbok can go without water for an unlimited period of time. It has a built-in 'radiator system' in its nasal passage which cools the blood on its way to the brain and thus largely eliminates the necessity for normal perspiration.

65 The thick fleshy leaves of the dollar bush, **Zygophyllum stapfii**, are eaten by springbok, mainly for their moisture. The stems are of a hard and richly coloured wood which dries into fantastically gnarled shapes and acquires a smooth satiny sheen as it is polished by the wind and sand.

66 As the wind blows sand grains, in this case garnet, quartz and magnetite, over the crest of the dune the difference in size and specific gravity produces these intriguing surreal patterns as the grains slide down the slipface.

IN A MODERN context the courage of the early explorers is beyond comprehension. What motivated them to go into the inhospitable, isolated and cheerless wastes of the Skeleton Coast, not knowing what awaited them, whether they would find water and without any means of communication with the outside world, is a question that only they could answer. I well recall the sudden constriction of the muscles in my throat and the distinct flutter in my heart, when on the return journey after my first trip to the Skeleton Coast in September 1977 the engine of our Piper aircraft refused to start after we had refuelled at Möwe Bay. The surroundings which up to then I had found so graphically beautiful all at once became bleak and godforsaken, and how far from civilisation we suddenly seemed to be! This was notwithstanding the knowledge that Ernst Karlowa of Nature Conservation was a mere 30 minutes' walk away at the Möwe Bay control post, and that we were in direct and immediate radio contact with Walvis Bay. I was overcome with awe and respect for early explorers such as Diego Cão, who, when he planted his *padrão* at Cape Cross, had ventured ashore on what must have been the most desolate stretch of shoreline he had ever set eyes on, and Georg Hartmann, the geologist from Germany, who had made several pioneering expeditions into the Skeleton Coast wilderness in an attempt to open it up to civilisation.

64

65

66

Rocky Point, the most well-known landmark on the Skeleton Coast, is frequently referred to by the early explorers, sometimes as Fort Rock.

According to Herodotus, the Phoenicians were the first sailors to circumnavigate the continent of Africa. The Egyptian Pharoah Necho II sent a flotilla of ships down the east coast and up the west coast of Africa in 600 B.C., which must have been a remarkable voyage, since it occurred more than 2 000 years before attempts were made by the Portuguese to find a route round Africa. Herodotus records that the journey took them three years and that they landed at various points en route, on some occasions long enough to plant and reap crops before resuming their voyage. It seems hardly likely, however, that they landed on the Skeleton Coast, as from a seafarer's point of view a less inviting or hospitable coastline is hard to imagine.

DIEGO CÂO'S CROSS

More than 2 000 years later, some six years before Christopher Columbus discovered the New World, King John II of Portugal launched the first voyage of exploration down the west coast of Africa. The intention was to search for the southernmost point of the African continent and then to navigate a sea route around it, in order to gain access to the rich spice trade of the East. This first voyage was undertaken by Diego Câo, a knight of the Portuguese court and navigator of some repute. Each of his two ships had on board a stone pillar or *padrâo*, hewn from the rock of Lisbon, which he was to erect on new-found shores in the name of Portugal and Christendom. This first journey took two

Opposite

67 Vehicle tracks are a major form of pollution in the Skeleton Coast Park. Restricting their occurrence is a constant conservation problem and one of the reasons why tourism is supervised in the wilderness section of the park.

115

years, during which time Câo extended the range of Portuguese navigation down the African west coast into uncharted waters beyond the Congo well into present-day Angola. He had planted the *padrões* at the mouth of the Congo River and at Cabo do Lobo or Seal Cape, the present-day Cabo de Santa Maria, north of Mossamedes in Angola. King John was far from satisfied and within eighteen months, in the second half of 1485, Diego Câo set off on the second of these pioneering ventures, again with instructions to find a route round Africa to the Indian Ocean and again with a *padrâo* on board each of his two caravels. He sailed past the furthermost point of his previous voyage, and must have cursed in frustration as the endless coastline persisted doggedly southwards instead of yielding to the east. He went ashore at Cabo Negro in southern Angola, erected the first of the *padrões*, and resumed his voyage, the shore through the mist and haze becoming increasingly desolate, dry and inhospitable. In December 1485, as his ships sailed past the mouth of the Kunene, a vivid splash of green in the otherwise bleak desert landscape, they entered Namibian waters for the first time. But the coastline still extended relentlessly to the south, and Câo's hopes of reaching Africa's southernmost tip must have virtually ceased by the time he made a landing at a small rocky cape projecting into the sea. Whether it was on account of the increasingly difficult weather conditions or possibly because he sensed that his end was near is not certain, but Diego Câo decided to erect his last cross at this point, which later became known as Cape Cross. Early in January 1486 the heavy stone pillar weighing more than half a ton was embedded in a supporting mound of rock and earth. It projected nearly three metres above its surroundings. On the front was engraved King John's latest coat of arms, while inscriptions in Latin and Portuguese on the reverse side read: 'In the year 6685 of the creation of the earth and 1485 after the birth of Christ the most excellent and most serene King Dom Joâo II of Portugal ordered this land to be discovered and this *padrâo* to be placed by Diego Câo, gentleman of his house'. Shortly after the two caravels had set sail for the return journey to Portugal, Diego Câo died, his ideal sadly unfulfilled. The exact circumstances of his death are not known, but the Skeleton Coast had claimed its first recorded victim.

For centuries Câo's *padrâo* stood in obscurity until it was seen by a certain Captain W. Messum, some time between 1846 and 1848, who was combing the waters of the Namibian coast in search of guano deposits and any other commercially viable products. He was aware that the Portuguese seafarers had navigated this coast some 400 years previously, and erroneously credited the cross to Bartholomew Diaz. In 1879, more than thirty years later, Captain W. B. Warren of the English cruiser *Swallow* noticed the cross while he was searching inshore for a landing-place, and correctly ascribed its date of erection to 1486. He was accompanying the *Christina* on a mission to land supplies at Rocky Point for the Dorslandtrekkers of the Kaokoveld, who were in dire straits and in desperate need of provisions and medical supplies. These boats could find no suitable landing-place on the inhospitable Skeleton Coast and eventually off-loaded the provisions a long way from the Kaokoveld, at Walvis Bay, where they were subsequently collected by grateful Dorslandtrekkers.

By this time Germany was about to take the first steps which led to her eventual complete annexation of the territory of Deutsch-Südwestafrika. The gunboat *Wolf* was dispatched by the German Admiralty to hoist the German flag at various points along the coast. Wooden noticeboards proclaiming the protection of the Reich were erected, one of which was in the vicinity of Cape Cross in August 1884, thereby supplanting after 400 years Portugal's claims to sovereignty. In a search for a suitable landing-site, Captain Becker of the cruiser

Falke came upon the *padrâo* at Cape Cross in late January 1893, to find that it had tilted and was lying towards one side. Realising that it was both vulnerable and of historical importance, he removed it and took it on board, with the intention of shipping it to Germany. As the *Falke* had to undergo repairs before setting out on the return voyage, Câo's *padrâo* was transported first to Cape Town, by a strange twist of fate accomplishing the mission which had eluded its erector more than 400 years earlier. The cross was finally delivered in Germany on 17 November 1893. It was first taken to the Naval Academy at Kiel and was then transferred to the Institut für Meereskunde in Berlin. After suffering bomb damage during a raid in the course of the Second World War it was restored and is now installed in the Museum für Deutsche Geschichte in East Berlin.

When the crew of the *Falke* removed the *padrâo* from Cape Cross they erected a five-metre-high wooden cross in its place. In January 1895 this cross was once more replaced by a granite replica of the original *padrâo*, brought all the way from Germany by another cruiser, the *Sperber*. In addition to the original inscriptions in Latin and Portuguese it now had the eagle of the German coat of arms and the following in German: 'Erected by order of the German Kaiser and King of Prussia Wilhelm II in 1894 at the place of the original which has been weathered through the years'.

Another interesting memorial which can be seen at Cape Cross is a simple slab placed on the ground near the present-day seal-processing plant. On it is inscribed the name and birthplace of one Martin Beheim, a German from Nürnberg, who was Diego Câo's navigator on his voyage of discovery in 1486. His birth and death are dated as 1459 and 1507, and the year when Diego Câo's cross was originally planted, 1486, is inscribed at the bottom of the slab.

A distinction which in pioneering terms also belongs to Cape Cross is that it was the first point in South West Africa from which a railway line was built. This was initiated by the rich guano deposits in the area which were discovered by the Englishman, Walter Matthews, in 1895. Matthews had been sent up the coast by the German Government to investigate reports of the fur seals at Cape Cross. In his report to his employers he made no mention of the deposits that he had found, but took the news of his find to England, which resulted in the formation of the Damaraland Guano Company. The company obtained a concession from the Deutsche Kolonial Gesellschaft, under the terms of which they could kill seals and work any guano deposits which occurred between the mouths of the Ugab and Omaruru Rivers. To work the guano deposits a locomotive and a complete railway were necessary, and thus the first railway line was constructed, with great difficulty, in 1895. It was in use for eleven years until the company stopped operations, after which it fell into disrepair. The dark outlines of the track and sleepers are still discernible on the salt-pans south of Cape Cross.

THE VOYAGE OF CAPTAIN MESSUM

An explorer-navigator to whom considerable reference is made in early accounts of Kaokoland and the Skeleton Coast is a certain Captain W. Messum. During the years 1846 and 1848 he undertook a voyage of exploration up the Skeleton Coast towards Angola and in his account makes mention of several familiar landmarks. It is certain that he went ashore at Cape Cross, and explored inland towards the Brandberg, which he called Mount Messum. The honour of having the renowned Brandberg named after him was, however, not to be his, although a lesser circle of mountains towards the west is now known as the Messum Crater.

Captain Messum was astonished to find traces of human beings in the area. At the foot of the Brandberg, or Dourissa as it was locally called, he found a village of Berg Damaras, which consisted of about fifty families, owning a number of sheep and goats. There were several water springs in the vicinity and the people appeared to eat mostly narra seeds and small bulbs, although it seemed game was plentiful: the huts were covered with gemsbok and other animal skins.

He continued up the coast, finding the forty kilometres north of Cape Cross the most interesting part of his exploring cruise. He was looking for a bay, which the Portuguese in their charts called Angra de Santa Ambrosia, as well as Hogden's Harbour, which had been discovered by the American sealer and explorer, Captain Benjamin Morrell, and which was reputed to be on that section of the coast. He gave up after fifteen days' search, however, having found neither. Hogden's Harbour was obviously a misspelt version of Ogden's Harbour, to which considerable reference is made in travel accounts, and which from the 1850s onwards appears on numerous maps of Southern and South West Africa. The said Captain Morrell named the harbour on a sealing voyage in his schooner, the *Antarctica*, in 1829. He had on board a William Ogden, a young man only 21 years of age, who drowned while sealing off the coast of Mercury Island, Spencer Bay, on Christmans Eve, 1828. Several months later the *Antarctica* sailed past Cape Cross and some kilometres to the north found an extensive reef of coral and lava rocks which formed a 'beautiful harbour of smooth water'. At the unanimous request of his crew Captain Morrell named it Ogden's Harbour, in honour of the ill-fated young man who had lost his life under such unfortunate circumstances. On the majority of maps, and as recently as 1978, Ogden's Harbour is placed north of the Ugab River mouth, in Ambrose Bay.

Captain Messum proceeded further north and it is clear from his descriptions that he was favourably impressed by the area surrounding the mouth of the Hoarusib River, where he observed much vegetation and driftwood on the beach. He mentions Rocky Point, which he refers to as Fort Rock Point, and a bay where he sought temporary anchorage, which he calls False Cape Frio, just south of which he had observed natives drying fish on stakes — probably a band of the now extinct Strandlopers, a nomadic race of beachcombing Bushmen. From Cape Frio he was unable to see much of the land as it had become extremely hazy, until he finally reached the mouth of the Kunene River. In early writings the Kunene is often referred to as the Nourse River, named by a certain Captain Chapman of the British warship HMS *Espiègle*, when he discovered it in 1824.

It is doubtful whether the Swedish explorer and naturalist Charles John Andersson ever penetrated as far as the Skeleton Coast proper, although he most certainly explored the eastern regions of Kaokoland. In his description of the Kaokoveld coast he relies on the observations of Captain Messum's voyage of exploration up the coast. Lawrence Green, however, in his book *Lords of the Last Frontier*, quotes Andersson as having said of the 'Coast of Hell': 'When a heavy sea-fog rests on these uncouth and rugged surfaces — and it does so very often — a place fitter to represent the infernal regions could scarcely, in searching the world round, be found. A shudder, amounting almost to fear, came over me when its frightful desolation first suddenly broke upon my view. "Death", I exclaimed, "would be preferable to banishment to such a country".' It is possible that this declaration refers to a portion of the coast south of Cape Cross. Nine years after his first attempt to explore Kaokoveld, Andersson returned and finally reached the Kunene River, fulfilling an ambition of seventeen years' standing. The many years of hardship and ill-health had caught up with him, however, and he died a few days later, at the age of forty. He was buried just south of the river.

ESSER, HARTMANN AND VON ESTORFF

In 1898 a book written by a certain Dr Esser, a German jurist, entitled *An der Westküste Afrika,* was published. Esser, who lived in Berlin, was wealthy, highly regarded as a colonist and in that year founded a large company for the purpose of promoting a colonial museum. In the book Esser describes a journey which he undertook from Cameroun in north-west Africa to Angola. He owned several large coffee and cocoa plantations in the vicinity of Viktoria in Cameroun, on which he was conducting experiments with various types of fruit. It would seem that he had aspirations to expand his activities to South West Africa. He describes an expedition which he undertook to the Kunene River on camels and riding oxen. He found the surroundings rich in game and records having seen a white rhino on the banks of the river. Travelling in a south-westerly direction along an old tributary of the river, they reached the sea where they found a bay, about two-and-a-half to three kilometres wide, which he named the Viktoria Augusta Harbour and placed on a map which he was preparing of the coast. This bay also became one of those elusive landmarks sought by subsequent explorers, such as Georg Hartmann, who was looking for a suitable location to establish a harbour. It is very likely that what Dr Esser conjectured to be a bay was in fact a shallow salt-pan filled with sea water, of which there are several to the south of the Kunene River mouth. It seems, however, that he found the land lying south of the Kunene River so formidable that he lost interest in any further explorations of South West Africa.

During 1894 and 1900 Dr Georg Hartmann, a geologist by profession, in the employ of the South West Africa Company, undertook several surveys of the Skeleton Coast, the most extensive of which was in 1896. Instructed by his company and in collaboration with the German Imperial authorities, he engineered a large-scale expedition to survey and map the Kaokoveld coast between Cape Cross and the Kunene mouth to seek out possible locations for the establishment of a harbour, and to investigate the occurrence of guano deposits. He was assigned a full complement of people to accomplish the task, local inhabitants as well as members of the Schutztruppe, among whom were Captain L. von Estorff, later to become a general of the German army, and Lts Helm and Volkmann. Von Estorff would survey the Uniab River, Helm the Hoab, Volkmann the Ugab and Hartmann the northern rivers, that is, the Hoanib, Hoarusib, Khumib, Sechomib, Nadas, Munutum and Kunene. In the course of this expedition the entire coastline, with the exception of the stretch between Angra Fria and the Kunene, and the river courses from east to west, were thoroughly explored. The river courses were used as 'bridges' by which to cross the desert towards the sea and the different parties would link up at appointed times in between the river mouths for further exploration of the coast.

Despite the careful positioning of base camps and provision stations at strategic points such as Sanitatas and Goabis in the south, and precautionary measures taken for the maintenance of their horses, oxen, travelling and luggage oxen, ox-wagons and tip-carts, they nevertheless had a number of close shaves. Hartmann recalled fourteen nerve-racking days that he had spent with the English mining expert, Pearson, the Swede, Captain Rosenblad, and Sergeant Frode of the Schutztruppe on one of the northern coastal sorties surveying the Sechomib, Nadas and Munutum Rivers. They ran out of food on this trip and in desperation resorted to baking a kind of bread concocted from the oats which they had taken along for the horses. Although they had painstakingly sieved the raw oats through the bottom of a butter tin into which they had made holes, they did not succeed in removing all the straw, with dire consequences to their digestive systems. They also found very little water along their route, which was not surprising, as 1896 had been an extremely dry year. Other than the perennial springs, which were few and far between, there was no natural water or grazing for the animals. On this northern expedition Hartmann and Frode rode with six horses from the camp at Nadas Spring overland to the Kunene, a journey which took them, including stops, a long 21 hours. They found no water on the way, although they saw plenty of game such as elephant, giraffe, lion, springbok, kudu, gemsbok and zebra, and at the Kunene their first crocodiles. They had intended following the river course to the mouth, and from there trying to locate the Viktoria Augusta Harbour, but their horses were in too poor a condition and they were forced to turn back. Another occasion that Hartmann remembered only too well was the night when they arrived at the mouth of the Sechomib River to set up a small temporary camp. It was cold and foggy and the south-west wind was blowing with gale force. Gigantic waves were breaking on the beach and jackals were calling in dismal and piercing tones. The driftwood was so wet that it was impossible to light a fire and sand was getting into everything; the tea, sugar, tobacco and food, their ears, eyes, noses and mouths; nothing was spared. To crown it all, their horses broke loose during the night. Prinz, one of the lackeys, was sent off to retrieve them. He returned only the following morning at 10 o'clock, having caught up with them almost halfway back to the main camp at Ogams, which is situated between 80 and 90 km from the Sechomib mouth as the crow flies.

It might be interesting to mention here that in 1878 a group of four Boers, headed by one Gert Alberts, had traversed the entire Kaokoland from east to west on horseback, going as far as 'Rotsfort' or Rocky Point on the Skeleton Coast, on an exploratory trip for the Dorslandtrekkers who were to follow later. Without the encumberment of wagons, animals and a large company, following the seasonal river courses and living off the land, they travelled with relative ease compared to the cumbersome German expeditions. Hartmann had much respect and admiration for the resourceful Boers, or farmers, who were so much more at home in desert country than the Germans.

That Captain Ludwig von Estorff was rather less impressed by the surroundings and its inhabitants than Hartmann is evident from a recent publication in which several of the letters that he wrote to his parents from South West Africa are published. He relates that near the mouth of the Uniab River where he pitched his camp he encountered a small group of Bushmen who lived from hunting and the fruit of the narra plant. Upon his question as to how they could live in such an odious environment, they expressed the opinion that far from being odious it was indeed a very beautiful place. Von Estorff recalled what Napoleon I had once exclaimed of the sandy environs of Jüterbock: 'And this the people call fatherland!' and realised that the Bushmen found the Uniab beautiful because it was their *heimat*, that is, their home. He found the fruit of the narra plant quite acceptable to eat, the flesh tasting rather like pear, except that it left a burning sensation on the tongue. Soon after he had pitched his camp the Bushmen, a group of about thirty, settled close by. He found them interesting company, but not particularly pleasing to the eye. The only tool that they used was a kind of knife which was made from whalebone rib, or sometimes elephant tusk, with which they peeled the narra fruit. When they occasionally caught a springbok to eat, they used a trap, as they did not seem to know hunting weapons.

Von Estorff relates with great admiration an occasion when Lt. Volkmann covered the 90 km between the mouth of the Ugab River and Cape Cross on foot. His horses had become ill due to the constant consumption of salt water, and he had sent them back to the base camp at Sorris-Sorris. In the company of a Mr Nitze, he set off for Cape Cross on foot. To make it easier to walk in the soft sand, he removed his boots on the way. The sun-heated sand burnt his feet so severely that he lay in bed for eleven days in the house of Mr Elers of the Cape Cross guano works. After he had recovered he again set out on foot, and walked the 110 km back to Sorris-Sorris, another severe ordeal on account of a shortage of water. Many of the problems that were encountered on the initial reconnaissance trips were due to inaccuracies on the maps. On one such a trip to the mouth of the Huab River Lt. Helm, finding no drinkable water, was obliged to turn back without resting. By the time he reached a usable waterhole his horses had been without water for four days, which surprised him greatly as up till then they had been under the impression that a horse could manage without drinking for only three days.

On another occasion, after a futile attempt to link up with Hartmann, Von Estorff, on his way back from the Hoanib River mouth to his camp in the Uniab River, almost lost his horses. While crossing a salt-pan all four horses simultaneously broke through the hard upper crust of salt and sank up to their bellies into the slush. Fortunately there was firm ground close by, but it took several hours of almost superhuman effort to pull them out.

Upon arrival back at camp, exhausted and very late, he received a message brought by a Bushman runner that Hartmann was unable to keep the appointment, as his horses were in too poor a condition to make the journey, but that he would travel along the inland route to join them. Plainly piqued, Von Estorff made the rather unfair comment that Hartmann was overcautious, and that he would do well to learn about courage from Helm and Volkmann.

While waiting for each other at various appointed places or resting their horses, they would often while away the time by playing chess. Von Estorff mentions an occasion at Sanitatas when a civilised two days were spent around a chess-board. Thus, when Hartmann finally arrived at Von Estorff's camp in the Uniab they, as on previous occasions, settled their differences over a chess-board. A few days later Hartmann and Captain Rosenblad set out for the coast in search of Ogden's Harbour. They failed to locate it, although they had found the exact spot that it was marked on the maps. As the coastline continuously changes it would seem that several of the bays marked by the early explorers had simply disappeared (probably because they had become sanded up).

Von Estorff complains that the water of the Uniab was very brack, and although he saw many tracks of game, he saw few animals. What is extremely interesting, however, is that he recorded having seen some quagga, animals closely related to Burchell's zebra, but with the striping considerably reduced, with bands only on the head and neck. One of them had come too close to the camp and had been caught by the dogs. He describes it as an attractive animal with an exceptionally large head, disproportionate to its small pony-like body. The hooves were small and sturdy, and it was remarkable how easily the animals could clamber up the steep walls of the river-bed. This was an extraordinary observation. According to Shortridge the last quaggas in the Cape Province had been killed off during 1865 and 1870, and in the Orange Free State between 1870 and 1873, possibly as late as 1878. The last living specimen had died in captivity in an Amsterdam zoo in 1883, and for all practical purposes quagga were regarded as extinct. There is little doubt from the description that what Captain von Estorff had seen were indeed quagga. His story is further substantiated by Jan Gaerdes' assertion that there were quagga in the vicinity of Swartmodder as late as 1922.

The attempt to locate the evasive Viktoria Augusta Harbour was deferred to the year 1900, when Hartmann and the engineer Toenessen set out on an expedition together. In this year the Otavi Minen und Eisenbahngesellschaft were seeking ways and means by which to export their ores, and were thinking in terms of building a harbour at and a railway line to the Khumib mouth. Hartmann was requested to investigate both possibilities, and set out on an expedition which consisted of himself, Toenessen and seventeen of the local inhabitants with an ox-wagon, two ox-carts, 70 draught oxen and nine horses. They left Outjo in July. It took them four weeks to reach Sanitatas where, on account of the water and grazing, they built their main camp. They came to the conclusion that, although building the proposed railway line was feasible, constructing a harbour at the Khumib mouth was not. This opinion was substantiated by a subsequent survey undertaken from the sea. Consequently the idea of building a harbour north of Swakopmund was relinquished, and eventually a railway line was built from Otavi through to Swakopmund. As they had also been instructed to look into the possibilities of constructing a harbour at Angra Fria and at the ever-evasive Viktoria Augusta Harbour, they then moved camp to the Nadas Spring, situated 70 km from the coast as the crow flies.

Their first attempt to reach the Kunene was not successful — they were unable to cross the high dunes and had run out of water. On a second attempt Hartmann took only the Hottentot, Josiah, and four horses. This time he managed to surmount the formidable dune belt that had thwarted him on the previous attempt, and was overcome with joy at the sight of the Kunene flowing peacefully like a wide silver belt through the fresh green reeds and rushes on the banks. Hartmann confesses to having had mixed feelings at the sight of this oasis. On the one hand he felt like an intruder, and on the other he regretted that so much sweet water was being lost to the colony. They proceeded down to the Kunene mouth and from there set off in the direction of Angra Fria. The waves were strong and the going was slow on that first day, and when they settled down for the night behind a small sand-dune it was cold, wet and stormy. The next morning they found themselves victims of a vicious sandstorm. (See extract from Hartmann's diary in the Prologue, p. 10.) The south-west wind had sprung up during the night, and not making any headway into the wind they were forced to veer off to the east and make their way back to Nadas. They lost their horses one after the other, until they were left with only Hans, a small dapple-grey animal, which, against all odds and over the most difficult of terrain without food or water for three days, held out until they reached Nadas. Hartmann had once more been thwarted in his attempt to traverse the portion of the coast between Angra Fria and the Kunene.

LAWRENCE GREEN AND THE CARP EXPEDITION

The well-known author and traveller Lawrence G. Green visited Kaokoland and the Skeleton Coast in the early 1950s with what was later to become known as the Carp expedition and gives an account of his experiences in his book *Lords of the Last Frontier*. It transpires that the expedition did not travel along the coast as had been planned, although it did reach Rocky Point, after the convoy had made its way down the Khumib River from Orupembe where the base camp was situated. Here they were overcome by a typical east wind sandstorm and were obliged to turn back. Nevertheless, the author gives many interesting accounts of

68

69

70

71

72

73

the people he met on this trip, several of which are relevant to the Skeleton Coast, or 'Coast of Hell', as he frequently refers to it.

The expedition was led by Bernard Carp, a Dutchman who had explored many parts of Africa and was a generous benefactor of museums. Dennis Woods, a mountaineer and ardent protector of wildlife and a person who had made frequent visits to Kaokoland, was honorary guide. The diamond prospector, Henry Voget, who had spent fourteen months prospecting for a diamond firm in the Skeleton Coast, also accompanied them. The company comprised in total fifteen white men of different nationalities and about the same number of local inhabitants who were employed as camp workers and assistants, and six vehicles consisting of trucks, vans and jeeps.

At Ohopoho (called Opuwa today), the official 'capital' of Kaokoland, Green was hosted by the Bantu Commissioner, Ben van Zyl, and his wife. Van Zyl visited the Skeleton Coast regularly. He once attempted to reach the Kunene mouth from his camp near the wreck of the *Dunedin Star*. He set off in a small jeep, but after he had covered about 100 km his battery failed and he was obliged to walk back to his camp with 'half a gallon of water, one tin of bully and one tin of beans'. He described the coast as 'the most hostile beach I have ever seen in my life'.

The base camp at Orupembe, 'the place where the plains begin', was situated about 65 km from Rocky Point. Not far to the west was Sanitatas, a Herero word meaning 'the place where the seeds come up', a waterhole of which the water, according to Green, had medicinal qualities. From there the party went on to meet the Tjimbas at Otjiu on the banks of the Hoarusib. The Tjimbas, ranked as a primitive people, are closely related to the Hereros. According to Dr N. J. van Warmelo, the then government ethnologist, a section of the Herero people migrated into the Kaokoveld from the north. They lost their cattle and became hunters and gatherers of such food as they could find and because they dug for their food like antbears, became known as the Tjimba or antbear people. After the Tjimba came more Hereros, who managed to retain their cattle. Most of these Hereros moved further south but a few remained, becoming known as the Himba or 'boasters'. The difference between the Tjimbas and Himbas is therefore one of poverty and wealth, with the Himbas having the cattle of which to boast.

While on this expedition Green also visited Sesfontein, or Zessfontein, meaning water from six fountains. Situated on the southern border of Kaokoland, it was the lost world or 'Shangri-La' of the Hottentot people. In earlier days Topnaar Hottentots, one of the oldest Nama tribes, who had lived for centuries in the vicinity of Walvis Bay, and the Swartbooi Hottentots, a tribe that had trekked up from the Cape after it was occupied by the Dutch East India Company, lived at Zessfontein. To escape the Hereros, the Topnaars and Swartboois had linked up and moved to Kaokoland in the 1860s and 1870s. After the uprising against the Germans in 1898, however, their numbers gradually dwindled to virtual extinction, and today the community consists mainly of Himbas, Hereros and Berg Damaras.

By far the most mysterious people whom they encountered at Sesfontein were the members of a group known to the Hottentots as 'Strandlopers', or as Green calls them, 'Sandlopers'. They were possibly the last of the Strandlopers, a Bushman race which inhabited the beaches of Africa centuries ago and has since become extinct. Anthropologists have stated that the original Strandlopers were beach-roaming Bushmen and not a distinct race. They were very small, dark, with matted peppercorn hair, wrinkled foreheads and deep-set eyes. Their speech was a

Opposite

71 Differential weathering gives these granitic gneiss rocks a weird and metaphysical quality as they stand like giant toadstools, melting in the scorching midday sun.

72 **Hoodia macrantha**, often called **ghaap** or **wildeghaap**, is eaten in its entirety by humans as well as animals, in particular black rhino, which probably accounts for its scarcity.

73 Dwarfed by the strong south-west winds, **Commiphora wildii**, one of the many **kanniedood** species, is typical of the coastal regions. When a twig is broken off it has a pleasant aromatic smell.

127

mystery, namely, Bushman language without the clicks. Since each click has a specific meaning, dropping them would appear to be more significant than merely 'dropping an aitch'. The Strandlopers lived mainly on the coast, subsisting on dead fish cast up onto the beaches, or dead seals, and when they were lucky, dead whales. They also ate shellfish which they cooked in ashes, making fires according to the Stone Age custom by twirling a small stick in a hole in a bigger one. When food on the beach became scarce, they would move inland and live off grass and leaves. They would even raid the stores of wild grain collected by ants from their anthills. They also caught field mice, lizards and insects and lived like other Bushmen off bulbs, roots and desert cucumbers.

At several locations along the coast there are 'settlements' of stone circles, thought to be remnants of Strandloper huts. The circles are between a metre and a metre-and-a-half in diameter, built from sharp stones pointing upwards. What the circles were actually used for has not yet been satisfactorily explained. Some of the daughters of the Strand- or Sandlopers married Hottentots and settled at Zessfontein. It is speculated that these Sandlopers might be responsible for the fine Bushman paintings in the caves of the Brandberg. Sandlopers called themselves 'Dauna-Daman', 'seaside people on a desert plain'. Their god was Damab, who lived in the sky and sent rains when he was pleased.

Green regretted that the planned journey up the coast from Rocky Point had not materialised, because it meant that they were unable to investigate the wrecks of certain wooden ships about whose origin there was much speculation. If the wrecks proved to be of Asiatic origin and were Arab dhows from the Indian Ocean, it could be an explanation to many mysteries, such as the cave painting of the 'White Lady' of the Brandberg and the Caucasian features and cultures found among some of the Hottentots. After meeting up with Fred Cogill, however, who had much experience of the coast, he felt that the mystery of the wrecks which had puzzled so many explorers was satisfactorily accounted for. Cogill was a retired policeman from Outjo and was manning the police post at Swartboois Drift where he had built the police station. He used to patrol the coast from the Kunene mouth to Cape Cross on horseback. During these patrols he came across a number of wooden wrecks, four of them well preserved, others almost buried in the sand. It was clear that Strandlopers had used some of the wood for their fires. In his opinion several of these wrecks were old American whaling ships, as he had found whaling gear, barrels for the oil and the small harpoons which they flung by hand. He also found a number of skeletons beside one wreck. It appeared to him that a whole crew had perished there, apparently from thirst. According to the skulls they were white men.

Cogill found a stone beacon at Cape Frio from where a track ran inland. This he followed for twenty miles until it ended in a large dune beyond which there was no trace of the road. He was of the opinion that the Portuguese had worked a mine there long ago. Cogill spent a total of fourteen years in Kaokoland and knew it better than any of the early explorers. He noted his discoveries and adventures in a series of diaries which were, however, unfortunately lost in a fire.

There is an interesting reference in Green's book to the eminent archaeologist, the Abbé Henri Breuil, a recognised world authority on rock art, who postulated some original theories about the famous 'White Lady' cave painting of the Brandberg. Abbé Breuil had met a prospector who claimed to have made a dramatic find on the Kaokoland coast. This man declared that he had seen a slab of stone bearing the inscription 'Golden Hind — Drake's Men'. It is just possible that the Kaokoveld prospector had seen a relic of Drake's famous voyage around the world towards the end of the sixteenth century.

THE VAN ZYL EXPEDITION

In 1954 the feasibility of building a harbour on the northern section of the coast was once again considered. This time the motivation was the development of the fishing industry towards the north, to supplement the already lucrative fishing industries of Walvis Bay and Lüderitz. For the first time the coastline from Swakopmund all the way to the Kunene River was going to be explored in motor vehicles. The entire trip was successfully completed over a period of twelve days and subsequently became known as the Van Zyl expedition.

It was on this expedition that the pitiful remains of what appeared to be a twelve-year-old child were found. Van Zyl and his party had just left the Hoarusib River when they happened on a deserted camp, which had apparently been used by a gang of diamond thieves. Nearby was a place where the presumed diamond gravels had been sieved. Sieves were lying around, and a great number of empty whisky bottles. Judging by the appearance of the camp the thieves had departed in a great hurry, leaving behind a lot of their equipment. To the one side there were some huts, in one of which the skeleton was found. It was clear that the child had not been buried. Indications were that it was not a white child, and hair lying next to the skull suggested that it had been a girl. Had she been left behind to die from hunger, or possibly murdered? They buried the bones, and on their return reported the incident to the police. Needless to say, this became another Skeleton Coast mystery that was never solved.

CANOE TRIP DOWN THE KUNENE

In 1965 adventurer and canoeist of some repute, Willem van der Riet, and Gordon Rowe, a man who had won the Pietermaritzburg/Durban canoe race, the Duzi Marathon, five times and the only person to have canoed down the Zambezi from Angola to the Indian Ocean, navigated the Kunene from its origin in the highlands of Angola all the way down to its mouth on the Skeleton Coast where, cutting through a gorge of about 550 m deep, it forges its way through the Baynes Mountains for about 160 km before reaching the Marienfluss. Initially, crocodiles were scarce, although from time to time they made their presence known by a rustle among the reeds and a ripple on the water. As Van der Riet and Rowe proceeded down the river, however, the numbers of crocodile grew and they became increasingly aggressive, snapping at the canoes and paddles. When the canoeists entered the Marienfluss Valley they had food left for four more days. The feared Kunene split now behind them, they were 350 km from Ohopoho (Opuwa) and 85 km from the sea. After leaving the Marienfluss they passed through the Hartmann Mountains, rapids following upon rapids, exhausting the two canoeists so that they frequently had to leave the river and carry their canoes overland. At one stage, in desperation, they carried their canoes into the desert in an attempt to return to the valley that they had left the previous day. Fortunately they came to their senses and returned to the river, where they climbed a cliff and to their intense relief saw the sea, barely more than 50 km away. At this point the river was still flowing through a narrow rock bed. On the southern bank dune sand was being blown endlessly from the desert into the river, while all that was to be seen on the northern bank were the grey rocks of Angola, but not a sign of life. Early the following afternoon a strong wind started blowing from the sea. They struggled for mile after mile, rapids following in quick succession. Just before the sun finally disappeared they saw a lonely

Portuguese outpost silhouetted in its last dying rays. The Portuguese were amazed, and somewhat suspicious, but when they realised that the two canoeists had come down the river, they overwhelmed them with Portuguese hospitality. Although Van der Riet and Rowe had to spend a number of days in hospital for their stomachs to recover from the ordeal of having gone without food for so long, by navigating the Kunene from its source to its mouth they had achieved the impossible.

The Wrecks

... when the elements prevail

TWELVE HEADLESS SKELETONS lying together on the beach, the bones of a child in an abandoned hut and a weatherbeaten slate buried in the sand with the message, 'I am proceeding to a river 60 miles north, and should anyone find this and follow me, God will help him', are evocative examples of the bizarre evidence of the many hapless people who came to their end on what must surely be the loneliest stretch of coastline in Africa. The message quoted here, dated 1860 and found in 1943, is telling confirmation of the invisible cordon which the coast has created to keep out intruders. The skeletons on the coast are not only those of men. The bleached bones of countless whales, exploited in the heyday of the whaling fleets, the sand and wind-blasted remains of tugs, liners, coasters, galleons, clippers, gunboats and trawlers, and their pitiful flotsam and jetsam, lie strewn untidily for endless miles of desolate beach, while at the river mouths in tangled heaps are the skeletons of a myriad trees, washed down from the interior by the floods of many seasons past.

The main cause of the plethora of shipwrecks along the Skeleton Coast is the ice-cold and fast-flowing Benguela Current with its deadly cross-currents, heavy swell and dense sea fogs, which become all-enveloping in an instant, reducing visibility to virtually nil. These factors, combined with gale-force winds that build mountainous waves, the treacherous reefs of coastal rocks, unexpected

Skeletons of ships on a lone beach bear out the name 'Skeleton Coast'.

shoals and sand-dunes that reach into the sea, unite the elements that sailors fear most in a frightening and all too real navigator's nightmare.

A story as told in *Die Voorgeskiedenis van Suidwes-Afrika* by Dr H. Vedder, which vividly illustrates the merciless and desolate nature of the Namibian coast, is that of Hembapu, a hero and leader of one of the roving bands of Hereros which frequented the countryside inland from Swakopmund. Game was plentiful and as an additional livelihood Hembapu and his followers stole the livestock of the Nama. Hembapu was tall and strong, the living was good and he and his followers rarely found it necessary to return to their native Kaokoveld. After one particularly devastating marauding expedition, however, the Namas resolved to stamp out the thieves of their cattle once and for all. Hembapu and his people were no match against the Nama with their metal-tipped arrows and assegaais and they were soon obliged to withdraw to the Kaokoveld. They decided against travelling through the interior, as they would have to pass the Berg Damara of the Erongos, who had no respect for the cattle of the Herero, and then the Paresis Mountains, which were inhabited by the San, a fierce tribe of Bushmen. Instead they set off along the beach, heading for the Omaruru River mouth, from where they would trek into the interior. As they approached the mouth of the river they saw in the distance two strange apparitions, and were first unsure as to whether they were seeing animals or humans. When they saw that the apparitions had only two legs they realised that they were human. As they came closer they perceived two white men, virtually naked and gesticulating wildly. On the beach nearby there was a stranded boat. The two white men joined them and partook

132

of the Hereros' sour milk. Soon after one of the men died. They attributed his death to the sour milk that he had drunk, on account of his not being accustomed to it. The other man wanted to accompany them to the Kaokoveld, but they were unwilling to take him and, presenting him with one of the stolen oxen, abandoned him to his fate.

Another legendary story is that of the lion at Okau Spring. A band of Herero from the interior of Kaokoland were travelling along the bed of the Munutum River towards the Skeleton Coast with their headman to collect salt from the Cape Frio brine-pans. They stopped at the Okau Spring to drink water. While they were resting there a lion charged them, bearing straight down on the headman. They heard a crash of thunder, the lion dropped dead, and a dishevelled, hairy and bearded white man appeared out of the reeds. They took him back to Kaokoland, but what became of him after that is not known.

THE VOYAGE OF THE MÖWE

In September 1884, a certain Captain Hoffmann of the sloop the *Möwe*, sailed up the coast of South West Africa, instructed by the German Imperial Authorities to seek out suitable landing-places north of Cape Cross and to hoist the German flag at strategic points. Where both S. M. S. *Wolf* and the English cruiser, the *Swallow*, had failed to find suitable landing-places north of Cape Cross, the *Möwe* anchored relatively easily at Angra Fria, north of Cape Frio, under the eighteenth degree of southern latitude. It is interesting to note that at that stage the northern boundary of South West Africa was the eighteenth degree of latitude and that it was only later moved to the Kunene River. After landing, Captain Hoffmann hoisted the German flag and erected a board with the words 'Imperial German Protectorate' at the bay. He makes the observation in his report that the surrounding land made a spectacular, wild and grandiose impression, but that the praise which certain travellers had expressed of the area, in particular the Swede Andersson and the Frenchman Father Duparquet, who had visited the Kaokoveld early in the nineteenth century, was decidedly overenthusiastic. Behind the bay he climbed a sand-dune and came upon an extensive, salt-impregnated sandy plain, on which there were sporadic rows of desert sand hills. Here he saw his first mirage. It seemed to him that the sand-dunes were inverted on the heated waves of air, while the mountains in the background were floating on a lagoon of water. The mountain chains towards the interior were at all times shrouded in a yellow haze of sand.

Shortly after resuming the journey, a few kilometres south of the bay, the crew of the *Möwe* detected a settlement on the shore. It consisted of a white tent or gable-shaped covering, a flagpole and several boats drawn up on the beach. Although the *Möwe* passed close by and raised her flag, no living creatures appeared. They could not land and strong winds eventually forced them to move further out to sea. The origin of the settlement remains a mystery to this day. On his journey back Captain Hoffmann found Ogden's Harbour particularly suitable as an anchorage, although it subsequently became sanded up to the extent that later explorers failed to locate it. North of the mouth of the Hoanib River he inspected a landing-place which he named Möwe Bay after his sloop. About ten kilometres north of Cape Cross he found the wreck of a large iron ship lying high up on the beach, a landmark which gradually disintegrated and disappeared with the passage of time.

THE RESCUE OF THE DUNEDIN STAR CASTAWAYS

The story of the rescue of the castaways of the *Dunedin Star* reads as a long, excruciating and frustrating series of endless disasters, with incredible hardship on the part of the castaways, unbelievable feats of valour on the part of certain individuals and a certain degree of inefficiency on the part of others. That only two lives were lost in the process is surprising, considering all the vehicles, vessels and aircraft involved, and the incredible odds. Maritime reporter John Marsh pieced the story together and published it in 1944 under the title *Skeleton Coast*, a highly successful book which soon became a best-seller and was subsequently reprinted in several different editions.

Opposite

74   The treacherous fog bank, typical of the Skeleton Coast, viewed from the roaring dunes south of Rocky Point.

All that is left of the **Dunedin Star**, wrecked in 1942 about 80 km south of the Kunene mouth, are the rusting remains of a fuel tank, part of the ship's cargo.

Late on the night of 29 November 1942, some kilometres off the Kaokoland shore about 40 km south of the Kunene mouth, the *Dunedin Star*, a British cargo liner of 13 000 tons, struck a shoal and ripped her bottom open. She was carrying 21 passengers, a crew of 85, mail, war stores consisting mainly of explosives, and a mixed consignment of war equipment. Rather than let the boat sink the captain ran her aground and radioed Walvis Bay, from where the message was relayed to Cape Town, and the wheels of a long and arduous series of rescue attempts were set in motion. Two ships, the British *Manchester Division* and Norwegian *Téméraire*, were instructed to proceed to the scene of the wreck. Their locations were, however, such that they would take two days to reach the stricken vessel. A South African Naval Forces' mine-sweeping trawler, the *Nerine*, and the South African Railways' tug, the *Sir Charles Elliott*, were dispatched simultaneously

75

76

77

from Walvis Bay, both of which would also take at least two days to reach the stranded ship.

On the morning of 30 November the Captain of the *Dunedin Star* decided to abandon ship. Towards the shore the scene which in the moonlight had seemed entrancing, almost romantic, was harsh and uninviting in the light of day, the peaceful lagoon in reality a waste of bleached white sand and the mountains in the background a barren expanse of endless sand-dunes. They were approximately 500 m from the beach and the surf was pounding and battering the vessel to such an extent that Captain Lee feared that it would soon break apart. He had only one motor-boat, which was rendered useless after three trips, during the course of which the passengers and 42 members of crew were taken ashore. Forty-three members of the crew were marooned on board, while the people on the beach, of which eight were women, three with babies, were stranded without shelter and with very little food and water. With the oars, mast and sails from the lifeboat a small shelter was built for the women and children. A search for water caused considerable distress when twelve headless skeletons were dug out from underneath the sand in the vicinity of some half-buried huts built from wreckage. There was nothing to identify the dead or their ship and no way of telling how they had met their end.

The remaining crew members tried unsuccessfully to reach the shore, and Captain Lee radioed Walvis Bay once again, requesting that an aircraft be sent to pick up the people from the beach. On the third day all four rescue vessels arrived. The 43 remaining members of crew were taken off the *Dunedin Star* by volunteers of the *Téméraire,* and transferred safely aboard the *Manchester Division*. The sea was, however, too rough for any of the four ships to attempt an approach to the shore. Radio messages were sent to Walvis Bay requesting that supplies of food and water be flown to the castaways on the beach. At this juncture the *Sir Charles Elliott* turned back for Walvis Bay, as it was running low on coal. The *Téméraire* had already left. Concern was mounting for the safety of the castaways on the beach and that evening the South West African Division of the South African Police dispatched a rescue convoy from Windhoek to reach the castaways overland. The convoy consisted of eight vehicles and was manned by the South African Defence Force led by Police Captain W. J. B. Smith.

By the fourth day the castaways were beginning to despair. The nights were extremely cold and the days unbearably hot. A relentless wind blew in from the sea and a fine sand penetrated everything. In the course of the morning the *Nerine* attempted fruitlessly to send provisions ashore, which the crew had tied to wooden rafts, but the strong current washed all their attempts northwards towards Angolan waters. By the afternoon the *Manchester Division* also left to return to Cape Town, as there was clearly nothing more she could do to help.

Earlier that morning a brand-new Lockheed Ventura twin-engined bomber piloted by Captain Immins Naudé left Cape Town, stopping at Walvis Bay to pick up the supplies that were to be dropped to the castaways by parachute. On his flight up the coast he was surprised to see the *Sir Charles Elliott* stranded in the surf, 300 m from the shore. The tug had been carried 20 km off course by strong currents and had run aground before dawn that morning. While the crew were still climbing into the lifeboat it had been torn away by a huge breaker and taken ashore with only three men on board. It was now washed up and useless on the beach. Seventeen men were still on the wreck with little hope of rescue as the tug had no radio to call for help. Captain Naudé radioed Walvis Bay, and as there was little else he could do, went on to the castaways of the *Dunedin Star*. He dropped his parcels of food, water and medical supplies and circled round to look for a suitable landing-spot, as he intended flying at least the women and children back to safety. He managed to land safely, but while taxiing became hopelessly bogged down in the loose sand, and had to radio that they, the rescuers, were now also in need of help.

On the morning of the fifth day the *Nerine* had to abandon the rescue attempt: by this time she only had sufficient supplies of coal to reach Walvis Bay. On the sixth day a second Ventura, flown by a Major J. N. Robbs, left Cape Town, landing at Walvis Bay for supplies. He found the *Sir Charles Elliott* still upright in the surf, with thirteen men on her bridge and six men and a small boat on the beach. Five of the seventeen marooned men had attempted to reach the shore in a frail dinghy but it had capsized. Three men had managed to swim ashore, one had managed to get back on the tug, and the fifth, the first mate, was carried away and never seen again. Robbs dropped supplies to the men on the shore and proceeded towards the *Dunedin Star*, where he dropped more supplies on the beach. He flew inland to see if he could locate the overland search party, but could not find it and returned to Walvis Bay.

On the seventh day another mine-sweeper, the *Natalia*, arrived at the scene of the wreck. She managed to float some supplies to the castaways, but had to turn back to Walvis Bay on account of engine trouble. By this time it was four days since the *Sir Charles Elliott* had run aground. Three more men, including a certain Mathias Koraseb, who had made it back to the ship after the second attempt to reach shore, struck out for the beach. All three men made it but minutes after being helped ashore by their shipmates, Mathias expired. He was buried in a crude grave, which was marked with a wooden cross. Many years later the Monuments Commission erected a brick and stone grave with an inscribed brass plate as a memorial. With the assistance of the two additional men the lifeboat was dragged back into the surf and the remaining crewmen taken ashore.

On the eighth day Robbs made his third trip to the castaways, dropped

Overleaf

78 The cool darkness of a desert night is dispersed by the dawn.

79 All that remains of a former delta of the Nadas — once a mighty river, today hardly recognisable as such — is a haphazard disarray of sand and rock. The black strip in the background is a brine-pan.

The red-brick grave of Mathias Koraseb of the **Sir Charles Elliot** that was erected by the Monuments Commission is rather out of keeping with the surroundings.

78

79

supplies and once more set off towards the interior to look for the rescue convoy, again without success. Two more Venturas, piloted by a Major Mathys Uys and a Captain P. S. Joubert, left for the scene, one from Cape Town and the other from Pretoria, while the *Nerine* was once again dispatched from Walvis Bay, this time equipped with a surf-boat and a specialised crew, to try another rescue attempt from the sea. On the ninth day the three Venturas again left Walvis Bay, Major Uys and Captain Joubert with supplies for the castaways, and Major Robbs to try and locate the overland convoy, which by now had been on its way for seven days and was causing serious concern in Windhoek. Uys dropped a message for the survivors of the tug, advising that eight of them should set out towards Rocky Point where he would attempt a landing to pick them up.

By this time Major Robbs had at last located the missing convoy. It transpired that after leaving Kamanjab, a small settlement north-west of Outjo, they had suffered an unbelievable series of mishaps and breakdowns. They had become endlessly bogged down in thick sands, some days covering only a few kilometres, and the fact that they had only one air-pump and no radio hampered them considerably. The one single pump, a hand one at that, had to service 34 tyres and earned the leader of the convoy the nickname of 'Pump' Smith.

On 3 December the news of the stranded tug and Captain Naudé's bogged-down Ventura had reached Windhoek, and a second convoy was sent overland, leaving on 5 December under the command of a Captain H. Borchers, to follow in the tracks of the first convoy. By 7 December the police chief in Windhoek, Lt. Col. Johnston, had become so worried that he personally set out in a police car, with several assistants and two light delivery trucks. Only after running into a fair degree of trouble himself and learning at Purros, a fountain in the Hoarusib River, that the convoy had passed through three days previously did he return to Kamanjab, in one vehicle, eight days later and five kilograms lighter in weight.

When Smith and his convoy arrived at Rocky Point on 8 December he was surprised to find the crew of the wrecked tug there as well. A Ventura dropped a message asking Smith to collect the rest of the crew and take them to Rocky Point, where aircraft would attempt to fly them to safety. Arriving there they found the two Venturas, Major Uys and Captain Joubert, who divided the crew between them and flew them safely back to Walvis Bay. From Rocky Point Captain Smith set off along the coast towards the castaways but soon found that the sand was too soft and loose, and drove inland to find harder ground.

On 9 December the *Nerine* anchored as close to the beach as she could, and rescued nineteen of the castaways that afternoon and another seven the next day. Forty-one people, including four airmen, still awaited rescue on the beach. On the eleventh day the *Nerine* was obliged to turn back for Walvis Bay and took the 26 people she had rescued to safety. By this time Smith's convoy was struggling through the Cape Frio salt-pans, and in addition to the fog had rain and freezing morning winds to contend with. On 12 December, the thirteenth day since the stranding, the convoy came to a dead halt about three kilometres from the castaways. Smith and the doctor, Captain Hutchinson, set out on foot and were received with uncontrolled joy. Early the next morning they set out on the return journey. After covering 10 km they met up with the Borchers convoy and after another four days arrived at Rocky Point where Major Uys was waiting. In two trips he managed to fly eighteen of the castaways to Walvis Bay, where they were hospitalised. All of them recovered from their ordeal, including a pregnant woman who gave birth to a normal baby a few days later. The two convoys set off with the remaining nineteen castaways for Windhoek, arriving there on Christmas Eve, 26 long and gruelling days after the *Dunedin Star* had run aground.

This was not the end of the story for Captain Naudé, who set out first by sea, and when that attempt failed, by air to salvage his bomber. A convoy of ten vehicles, 27 men and a caterpillar tractor, which took nine days to reach the plane, managed to get it out of the sand after four frustrating days. With a crew of two Naudé took off on 29 January 1943, but 45 minutes later the starboard engine seized and the Ventura took a nose dive into the sea. Deep down the heavy engines broke loose and the fuselage surfaced again. The three airmen, battered and bruised but alive, struggled into the fuselage and, when it drifted ashore and lodged itself on a rock, climbed out and waded through the surf and onto the beach. As they had no communication with the salvage convoy or with their base in Walvis Bay they soon realised that their only hope was to try and intercept the salvage party before it reached Sarusas Fountain in the Khumib River. Somehow, despite their injuries and probably driven by desperation, they managed to cover the 50 km on foot in less time than it took the salvage party to travel 110 km and, travelling with them, arrived in Windhoek six weeks after they had started out on their doomed attempt to salvage the plane.

OTHER WRECKS OFF THE SKELETON COAST

The Portuguese mail steamer, the *Mossamedes*, ran aground in a storm off Cape Frio early in 1923. Formerly the *Sumatra* of the P&O Line, it left Lourenço Marques, or Maputo as it is known today, on a significant date: it was Friday, the 13th of April, 1923, and she was en route, via Cape Town, to the Angolan ports and finally Lisbon. There were 258 people on board when she left Table Bay, four of whom were convicts. With the exception of fourteen blacks and two Englishmen, the rest were Portuguese. The ship was carrying a dangerous cargo, which included 25 cases of gelignite, several cases of detonators and fuses, and a number of drums containing sulphuric acid. Some time after midnight on 24 April a message reading 'ashore Cape Frio _ _ _ S.O.S.' was received in Cape Town. This was the entire message and it was recorded from ship to ship on the open seas. It was the last signal heard from the *Mossamedes*.

Twenty-seven hours later the master of the Commonwealth and Dominion liner *Port Victor* reported that his ship had reached the waters round Cape Frio and that he had seen the *Mossamedes*, but that all her lifeboats were gone and there was no sign of life on board. Other than the stern which was rather deep in the water there was nothing to suggest that the liner had stranded. He could see no sign of an attempted landing on the shore. It looked as if the ship's entire company had been swallowed by the sea. In the meantime other ships were searching the seas between Cape Frio and the port of Mossamedes for survivors. Eventually a message was received that 227 of the missing company of 258 had been saved, while the fate of the missing 31 was solved a few days later. Eight lives had been lost when abandoning ship and the last of the seven lifeboats which were heading northwards had capsized and the 23 people on board lost. The remaining six lifeboats had been driven on at a speed of over five knots by a gale wind towards Port Alexandre, where they were met by fishing schooners which had been warned of the disaster. Two steamers were sent to Cape Frio to salvage the wreck, but salvage proved impossible, and it broke up soon after the disaster.

On the night of 1 November 1941, roughly over a year before the ill-fated wrecking of the *Dunedin Star*, about 300 km north of Walvis Bay, the British freighter, the *Bradford City*, was struck unexpectedly by a torpedo, resulting in a severe hole in her side which caused her to start filling up rapidly with water. Two

Overleaf

81 A swing of eroded magma gravel lends a graphic quality to the foothills of the Agate Mountain of Cape Frio.

82 The lower reaches of the Sechomib River gradually being invaded by a field of brack-bush dunes.

81

83

82

Previous page

83   The slipface of a large barchan dune with its ornamental pattern caused by a rare local shower makes a striking desert amphitheatre.

lifeboats were immediately lowered on the leeward side and 21 crew members managed to embark before the ship sank, forty minutes after having been hit by the torpedo. Chief Officer Louttit in the second boat, with supplies for nine days, a chart, sextant and a compass, headed south. There were thirteen people on board and it soon became apparent that they would not succeed in reaching Walvis Bay and would have to make for shore as soon as possible. It was nine days before they sighted land and another twenty-four hours before the surf was calm enough for them to land, 11 km north of the Ugab River. They pitched camp and the next day the two fittest men set off for Walvis Bay. As they were leaving, a South African Air Force reconnaissance plane saw them and dropped them iron rations, returning later with water and other supplies. When the news of the survivors reached Walvis Bay arrangements were made that twenty men from the South West African Infantry under the command of a Captain Richardson set out in four troop carriers to bring the stranded men back to safety. The convoy struggled through the night and finally got bogged down in the thick sand of the Ugab River mouth. Carrying the boatswain on a stretcher, the survivors were taken to the troop carriers from where they set off for Swakopmund. It was learned later in the week that the rest of the crew of the *Bradford City* in the lifeboat under the command of the Master, Captain Paul, had headed north and reached Lobito Bay in Angola safely. With the prevailing wind and the current in their favour they had had a less eventful trip than the men in the other lifeboat.

In the early hours of 11 November 1966 the *Viente e Oito de Maio*, meaning simply the 28th day of May, the date of Portugal's Independence Day celebrations, ran aground about 5 km north of Toscanini. She made contact with the radio station at Walvis Bay and, giving her position incorrectly, relayed that she was stranded on the rocks about one kilometre off the coast, had 30 men aboard and that they were unable to put out their lifeboats. The captain requested a lifeboat to take his crew ashore. As the message emphasised urgency, a police Alouette helicopter was dispatched from Windhoek, with Major G. J. J. Brand, District Commander of the South African Police at Walvis Bay and Port Captain Bob Harding on board. Shortly after the ship had run aground the men in the mining camp at Toscanini were alerted and Colonel Jack Scott and Ben du Preez went to the scene in trucks, taking with them a mobile electric plant, setting up lights to let the crew know that help was at hand. At daybreak an attempt was made to lower a lifeboat with twelve men aboard, but they were thrown out before reaching the water. Three managed to climb back on board, six reached the shore, but three were drowned. At this stage the helicopter arrived, and taking three crew members per trip flew all the men safely ashore. Initial ideas to try and save the ship were abandoned when the weather conditions deteriorated to such an extent that it became impossible, and yet another wreck was added to the grim list of trophies taken by the Skeleton Coast.

That modern technology in the form of radio communication, helicopters and four-wheel-drive vehicles, the presence of mining and prospecting companies and in latter years Nature Conservation personnel on the Skeleton Coast has done much to lessen the plight of victims of shipwrecks, leaves no doubt. One evening late in 1967 the seven o'clock news bulletin broadcast the information that a distress signal had been received by the Walvis Bay radio station to the effect that a fishing vessel, the *Catania*, had sprung a leak just off Cape Frio, was sinking rapidly and that the crew intended running her aground before she sank. After this one message all contact was lost. It was a cold night, the south-west wind was blowing, and the sea fog was lying heavily on the coast. Ernst Karlowa, who was then in the employ of the Sarusas Development Corporation doing harbour research at Möwe Bay, was requested by one of the directors of the Corporation to drive up the coast and try and find them. He set off at about nine o'clock, taking with him blankets and provisions, and after a difficult and hazardous journey along the beach found the men at two o'clock the next morning, wet and half frozen, as they had swum ashore after their ship had run aground. Karlowa took them to the old Cape Frio weather station where they spent the rest of the night in relative warmth and comfort before being taken to Walvis Bay.

The following story is undoubtedly the only one on record where the stranded crew of a shipwrecked trawler was saved on account of black rhino. In the course of 1973 Bernabé de la Bat, then Director of the Department of Nature Conservation and Tourism, Adolf Brinkman, then Member of the Executive Council charged with Nature Conservation, Dr Piet Koornhof, then Minister of Mines, and their pilot went on a flying trip to the Skeleton Coast to discuss the problems of the newly proclaimed Skeleton Coast Park. De la Bat wished to convince Koornhof that prospecting and mining in the area should no longer be allowed to continue. By showing him the extent of the damage already done by mining, and especially prospecting, he hoped to prove his point. On their way to Rocky Point they saw a motor vehicle driving down from Orupembe towards the coast. At De la Bat's request the pilot flew low to take the number of the vehicle and saw that it belonged to the Department of Bantu Affairs. It was clear that the occupant of the vehicle was on a fishing jaunt, and had entered the park unlawfully. Since its proclamation in 1971, anyone entering the park had to be in possession of a permit. Initially, it had been De la Bat's intention to send one of his nature conservators to apprehend the transgressor. Then he had second thoughts and decided against this, as there were a number of black rhino in the vicinity of Opuwa which he wished to translocate to the Etosha National Park and for which he needed the co-operation of the Department of Bantu Affairs. By apprehending one of the Department's officials for illegal entry into the park he might well cause friction and thereby jeopardise his negotiations concerning the rhino. This decision probably saved the lives of the crew of an American tuna boat, the *Islander,* which, unbeknown to De la Bat and his party had in the meantime run aground about 100 km north of Rocky Point. The crew had reached the shore safely, but as their radio was not functioning they were unable to summon help. The captain and the first officer started walking southwards and when they finally, in a state of utter exhaustion, reached Rocky Point they came across the trespassing fisherman. He had a radio in his vehicle, was able to inform the police and arrangements were made to have the stranded men rescued. Had it not been for a conservator's love of rhino, the story might well have had a tragic ending.

Despite modern technology, the Skeleton Coast remains as inexorable as ever and often still has the edge on those who venture on her shores. In 1973 the crew of the *Islander* found themselves in dire straits because their radio had ceased to function. In December 1976 the *Suiderkus,* a Cape Town-based trawler which had cost R3,5 million to build and was equipped with the most up-to-date navigational equipment, ran onto the rocks at Möwe Bay on her maiden voyage. The expensive electronic equipment had left her in the lurch and reduced her to being part of the scenery, a picturesque but temporary landmark. Battered by the waves and the passage of time her huge bulk has gradually broken apart, the hull deposited high on the beach one stormy night. Until she finally disintegrates completely, she will serve the rest of her time as a cormorants' perch and a topical theme for photographers.

Overleaf

84 Tinted orange by lichen-encrusted gravel, a vast open plain fades into a distant mountain range.

85 Ghost crabs are fair-weather creatures and when the sun is shining make their appearance in large numbers on the beaches. They live in holes about 20 cm under the sand and feed mainly on carrion and young mussels.

Aircraft and Other Mishaps

...when technology fails

IT WAS AN aircraft mishap that gave the Skeleton Coast its descriptive and appropriate name. In 1933 the Swiss pilot, Carl Nauer, on a flight from Cape Town to London, disappeared somewhere along the Namibian coast. He had last been heard of when refuelling at Walvis Bay before proceeding northwards. He was subsequently reported missing, the alarm went out, and a sea, land and air search was launched. Sam Davis, veteran Namibian journalist and correspondent for Reuters and the *Cape Argus* at the time, was covering the event. He suggested that Nauer had probably crashed into the sea or desert and that his bones might one day be found on the 'Skeleton Coast', the graveyard of ships and men. Nauer and his plane were never seen or heard of again, but a name for the loneliest beach in Africa had been coined, and soon became officially accepted.

Although the Skeleton Coast has become more accessible as a result of modern technology, and rescue operations are far more effective and streamlined today than at the time of the *Dunedin Star* rescue attempt in 1942, the elements still frequently gain the upper hand. The main cause of aircraft disasters is fog and the resultant lack of visibility. However well-equipped and technically advanced modern vehicles may be, the danger of becoming bogged down, whether on the beach, in a river-bed or driving across a brine-pan, is ever present. Becoming lost, especially when on foot, is always a hazard, and happens even to the local people.

Louw Rabie, a geologist of considerable repute, who in the late fifties was a member of Jack Levinson's prospecting team, was doing sampling on foot in the maze of mountains south-west of Sesfontein. He was assisted by one of the locals. One afternoon they had an arrangement to work separate routes and to meet later at an appointed place. The assistant never made his appearance. The police and specialised Bushman trackers searched the area thoroughly. From the way in which he had walked it was clear that he had lost all sense of direction and had become hopelessly lost. His tracks were visible only up to a point, from where the terrain became so rocky that they disappeared. He seemed to have vanished into thin air; what had become of him was never established.

AIRCRAFT DISASTERS

One misty morning Jack Levinson and his pilot, Tim Theron, took off from Levinson's Camp north of the Hoanib River. They had just become airborne when the wing of their Navion hit a shrub-coppice dune, causing them to turn a complete cartwheel back onto the airstrip. Mr Levinson and the pilot climbed out shaken but unhurt, but the Navion was a total write-off. More than twenty years later fate played one of her strange tricks when Theron, who had since left Namibia and joined the South African Air Force, while on a mission to the Skeleton Coast, died unexpectedly of a heart attack at Rocky Point.

Another South African Airforce pilot who came to his end on the Skeleton Coast was a certain Lt. Winterbach. At the time he was seconded to the South African Police Force to fly one of its Alouette helicopters. During 1966 he was requested to fly to Terrace Bay to link up with a police patrol that was on its way down from the Kunene. They had an appointment to meet at Terrace Bay in the afternoon, but by eight o'clock the patrol had still not arrived. Winterbach, another policeman and three officials of the Consolidated Diamond Mining Company, decided to go and look for them in the Alouette. The fog was lying low on the ground when they took off. As they banked over the sea to turn northwards they hit the water and the aircraft exploded. All five men were lost, none of the bodies ever being recovered.

Taking off in foggy conditions has caused many unnecessary disasters. During 1982 a well-known Windhoek personality, Piet Gouws, who was the managing director of SWABANK at the time, was lost under similar conditions. He took off in his Cherokee 300 from Terrace Bay into the fog just before sunset, and was never seen or heard of again. It was thought that he had possibly mistaken the time by one hour and was under the impression that he still had an hour and ten minutes of daylight to reach Henties Bay.

An amusing story which could well have had serious implications is that of how Dirk Mudge, one of Namibia's foremost political leaders, lost his Piper Cherokee on the Skeleton Coast. He was spending the weekend with a group of friends at Möwe Bay. They decided to go to Rocky Point for some fishing and prepared to set off in three light planes. Two of them had already taken off when Mudge found that the battery of his machine was flat. When he was unable to start it one of the other aircraft turned back and landed, by which time Mudge and his passengers had climbed out and were attempting to start the engine by swinging the propeller. It suddenly jumped to life and, although the handbrake was on, started running around in ever-widening circles. There was simply no way

Overleaf

86 A wild green-hair tree, **Parkinsonia africana**, in this case inappropriately named, takes a solitary stand in the Hartmann Valley.

87 A battered acacia holds its own in the bed of the Hoarusib River. When the river comes down in flood the high sand walls on its southern banks rumble impressively as their base is carried away underneath them, and sudden cascades of sand plunge down the slipface.

they could stop the plane. Although they hung on to the wings and tail, it kept going round like an enraged bull. The six people on the ground scattered in all directions, but there was no building on the ground or any other place behind which to hide. As one of them put it, 'There I was standing with the damn thing bearing down on me and I didn't even have a shotgun!' That the plane did not hit anyone was short of a miracle. It finally ran head-on into the other machine, which still had its engine running, and the two aircraft literally chewed into one another, ripping the petrol tanks apart and slicing the two propellers into tiny pieces of flying shrapnel. That they did not catch alight was another miracle, although, needless to say, both were very badly damaged. The pilot of the third plane, who had witnessed it all from above, must have felt that he was looking at a rather nightmarish cartoon, all over in less than three minutes.

In 1966 the well-known German writer of travelogues, Hans Otto Meissner, visited the Sarusas Development Corporation research station at Angra Fria. On the day he was due to return it was extremely windy, and there was a question as to whether their departure should not be deferred until later as they were travelling in a high-wing aircraft, which tends to be unstable on the ground when it is very windy. They eventually decided to take off, however, with two people hanging on either wing as the plane was taxiing. Just as the pilot opened the throttle for take-off, a sudden gust of air toppled the machine over so that it stood upright, with its nose buried in the sand and its tail pointing up to the heavens. The passengers were helped out and the machine put back on its wheels again, miraculously with no damage to its propeller.

Going round in circles really does happen in the desert. On this same trip Meissner and a guide left on a sightseeing tour to Orupembe from the camp at Angra Fria. The fog was particularly dense and lying low on the ground. Although the guide knew the area very well, after one and a half hours' driving they found themselves back at the very point from which they had started.

During 1976 the Navy research vessel, the S.S. *Protea*, was conducting a hydrographical survey of the coastline. The depth soundings were made with the assistance of radio beacons on land, and these were set up and moved by a land team which was taken ashore every day by an Alouette helicopter piloted by a South African Air Force pilot. The land team and a motor-cycle with which they travelled from one beacon to the next were deposited at strategic places each day. One day, after the land team had been taken ashore, the helicopter developed engine trouble on its flight back to the S.S. *Protea*, and was unable to return to pick them up. Ernst Karlowa, who was manning the Nature Conservation control post at Möwe Bay, was contacted by radio and requested to go to their aid. They were stranded about 50 km south of the Kunene River mouth without food, water or shelter. Karlowa left at once and, driving through the night, arrived the next morning to find them cold and downcast, having spent an extremely uncomfortable night on the beach.

On his way north Karlowa had come across a brand-new police pick-up truck bogged down in the brine-pans adjoining the beach north of Angra Fria. The police, travelling along the beach, had been returning from a patrol to the Kunene River. The tide came in before they could salvage the vehicle and it became completely submerged. At low tide it can still sometimes be seen. Karlowa recalls that the sight of the sunken police truck had made him put his foot flat on the accelerator, pray and drive straight ahead, not daring to look backwards when he felt his own vehicle sinking, but somehow lurching forward again just as it seemed to get stuck.

88 The blue of the Atlantic Ocean is an effective backdrop for this intricate pattern of interlaced barchan dunes photographed from the air.

THE HAZARDS OF DRIVING AT THE COAST

Driving across a brine-pan can be particularly hazardous. The top salt crust consists of 6-10 cm of hard surface, while underneath there is a slush with a porosity of 20 per cent, that is, a consistency of 20 per cent water and 80 per cent sand. When you drive over the crust it is likely to break, and the best thing to do is put your foot flat on the accelerator and, like Lot's wife, not look back, because if you do you will see that your vehicle is literally making waves like a speedboat in water. This can be quite frightening, enough to make you stop, in which case you are bound to sink into the slush and it could take days to get out. You cannot use a jack, because there is nothing to support it and as fast as you dig away the slush, it fills up again. Heavy equipment such as bulldozers would simply sink away and gradually disappear, as some of the pans are up to 100 m deep.

The rivers that come down in sudden flash floods can be equally hazardous. A vehicle of Rudolph Klein, well-known salt magnate of Swakopmund, was lost in the Hoarusib River when it came down in flood after the big rains of 1963. Some of his assistants were on their way from the Sarusas amethyst deposit to Swakopmund and had stopped in the river-bed to load something onto their vehicle. The river came down unexpectedly and promptly washed it away. The half-buried wreck of the jeep could be seen for many years afterwards. In 1968 a land-surveyor lost his vehicle in much the same way. He had decided to risk crossing the river, as it seemed to him that the floodwaters had subsided sufficiently. But then, as the Hoarusib is wont to do, it came down suddenly in a large 'wave', and the vehicle was washed down into the sea.

Nor is experience an infallible guarantee against this kind of disaster. During 1982, my husband, who has been driving in the area for more than twenty years, lost a Landrover on the beach. He was on his way to Cape Frio with a group of tourists at low tide and hit an unexpected patch of coarse mussel sand. The vehicle sank down up to its belly but, unperturbed, he tried pushing it out, and when this failed, still unperturbed, jacked it up onto planks. However, it simply drove off the planks and sank even deeper into the sand. By this time the tide was coming in rapidly and he was forced to abandon the vehicle to the elements. Within three hours it had toppled over on its side, become totally submerged, washed out into the sea and was tossed back onto the beach by the waves. By the time the tide receded again it was buried so deeply that it was impossible to dig it out, and at low tide it can be seen to this day. Nature Conservation personnel at Möwe Bay were alerted by radio and Slang Viljoen, who at the time was doing research on the elephants of the Hoanib River, drove the 200 km up the coast to come to the rescue, and took the stranded people back to their camp. About a month later a Nature Conservation vehicle was lost in exactly the same way, just north of the Hoarusib River mouth.

In 1975, when Angola became independent, a large number of Portuguese refugees, not knowing that they were entering an uninhabited wilderness, crossed into Namibia at the Kunene River mouth. At the time there were rumours that a boat with war orphans was travelling south to Walvis Bay, but that it had gone missing. Nature Conservation officials patrolled the coastline but could find no sign of it. It was suspected that the boat might have been intercepted by a Russian vessel. In September of that year Max Kessler of the 112 Squadron, who had been flying along the coast looking for signs of this boat, saw a large number of Portuguese vehicles crossing the Kunene River by pontoon into the Skeleton Coast. To attract attention the refugees, using stones, had spelt the word 'help'

on an incline. Ernst Karlowa of Nature Conservation and Colonel Koos Myburgh of the South African Police went to the rescue in four-wheel-drive vehicles. They found 66 vehicles, loaded to the hilt, carrying approximately 200 people, in the process of crossing the river, convinced that they would find a road to civilisation on the other side. The majority of the vehicles were saloon cars of different shapes and sizes. There was even a Mini among them. After a journey of many trials and tribulations which lasted six days, assisted by Super Frelon helicopters of the South African Air Force, 64 of the vehicles, driving along the beach at low tide and towed through the difficult spots by the four-wheel drive vehicles of the rescuers, managed to reach Möwe Bay, from where there was a road further south. The 120 women and children had been flown from the Angra Fria camp to Walvis Bay by helicopter.

Where a modest two-wheel-drive Mini made it down the coast, two sophisticated and expensive vehicles built especially for desert driving did not. During 1968 an international oil-prospecting company conducted an off-shore geophysical survey along the coast. They were exploring the continental shelf for possible oil deposits, working according to a gridiron pattern, correlating their position at sea with beacons set up by a team on land. The land-based team was using two Unimogs, reputed to be the strongest and most reliable desert and sand vehicles in the world. Just north of the seal colony at Cape Frio, however, the Unimogs got bogged down in the sand at low tide and, despite every attempt to free them, dug themselves deeper and deeper into the sand until finally the tide came in and took them away. The two 'unconquerable' vehicles were never retrieved.

Nevertheless, although shipwrecks still occur and vehicles still break down from time to time, nowadays there is a good chance that the occupants will be rescued, whereas a hundred years or more ago the chances were very remote if not non-existent. On a lonely stretch of brine-pan to the north of Angra Fria embedded in the salty crust of the pan's surface are the remains of a wooden cart, built by a small party of castaways, who were apparently stranded off Angra Fria. They had built the cart from wreckage, cutting the wheels with a knife out of wooden planks. They presumably packed such possessions and food supplies as they had on the cart and set out in a northerly direction, probably heading for the Kunene. Whether they were rescued or what became of them is not known.

Also unresolved is the mystery of the crouching skeleton found buried upright in a metre-deep grave, which was blown open by the wind, about 300 paces north of the *Dunedin Star* wreck. It is conceivable that the unfortunate occupant of this lonely grave was caught in a sandstorm and, to escape from the freezing wind and stinging sand, dug a hole in which to shelter, only to become buried alive before he realised what was happening to him.

Prospectors, Miners and Fortune Hunters

. . . the lure maximal, the yield minimal

DIAMOND PROSPECTORS ARE a breed on their own. They are romantics, born optimists, the most positive of thinkers, and gamblers by nature. They are prepared to suffer great hardship for the big bonanza that they believe will come their way. Those who came to the Skeleton Coast were no exception. The question was not whether there would be diamonds, but rather how best to dispose of them once they had found them, since there was no doubt that they were there. The area has exactly the kind of magnetism that attracts people such as these. Its geographical remoteness, the fact that entry has been restricted since 1907 and the discovery of rich diamond deposits at Alexander Bay and Oranjemund did much to create and perpetuate the myth that somewhere along the coast there lay untold wealth. The fact is that certain kinds of people will always believe in these legendary mineral riches, if for no other reason than that they want to.

When the Kaokoland was declared a prohibited area it was not, as many thought at the time, to prevent the discovery and exploitation of diamonds by private individuals. It was mainly to relieve the police of the necessity of patrolling the long waterless wastes, but also to create a cattle-free zone to expurgate the lung sickness that had been spreading from Angola. Strangely enough this seemed to add to the attraction, and time and again adventurers would risk their lives by entering the area illegally to search for diamonds. In many instances they were followed, tracked, arrested and convicted, but this again, rather than serving as a deterrent, added to the magnetism. Some of these fortune hunters never returned, as is evidenced by the human skeletons and unmarked graves which were found in the vicinity of deserted prospecting camps.

It was not only diamonds that made people risk their lives, or not ostensibly so. The late Jannie Peters-Hollenberg, an adventurous farmer from the Keetmanshoop district, had heard that there was a large quantity of whisky on the wreck of the *Dunedin Star* that had not been salvaged. This was in 1946, just after the war, when whisky was virtually unobtainable. Landing on the beach in his small Piper Cub tandem plane, he made several retrieval trips between the wreck and a farm in the Outjo district which bordered on east Kaokoland, where he kept a supply of aircraft fuel. By this time the ship was lying near the beach and, using the many motor-car tyres that lay strewn around, he was able to build a kind of staircase up to the ship at low tide. The tanks of the Piper Cub could hold sufficient fuel for only a single trip. On his way to the wreck a supply of fuel for the return journey would be packed on the back seat, while on the way back it was stacked with whisky. He made several trips but, although rewarded with a fair supply, he had to pay so much in tax to Customs and Excise that financially it was no longer worth his while and he stopped the trips. His late father, who in 1903 had been appointed as the first Mining Commissioner for South West Africa, had given him several maps on which were indicated possible and suspected diamond deposits. So, whether he risked his life for the love of whisky — which is unlikely since he was virtually a teetotaller — or for the love of diamonds, or possibly simply for the love of adventure, as he had done quite a bit of scouting around while he was there, he was fortunate that he had not come to any grief and lived to tell the tale.

THE DIAMOND HUNTERS FROM THE THEODORA

Shortly after the Kaokoveld had been declared a diamond area in 1929 a syndicate of diamond hunters made a daring entry from the sea into the forbidden zone, in an exercise which nearly cost them their lives. They set out from Cape Town, where they had made arrangements with a certain Charles Broker, the owner of a ketch, the *Theodora*, to land them on the Skeleton Coast. They claimed that they were in possession of details of a rich occurrence of diamondiferous gravel situated north of the Hoanib River. Unbeknown to them, however, the police had somehow come to hear of their intentions and were keeping an eye on their movements. They left Cape Town early in October 1931, but were plagued with misfortune from the outset. The mate was inexperienced, and the six diamond hunters were complete novices as sailors and useless as deck hands. After several close shaves they managed to reach Walvis Bay, where they replenished their supplies and set off northwards. When they reached the mouth of the Hoanib River, which was as far as Broker had contracted to take them, they saw signs of smoke on the beach and decided to go ashore. Two of them set out in a dinghy with a supply of food and water, but being completely inexperienced, they reached the shore only with great difficulty, losing their provisions in the process. The weather deteriorated to the extent that they were stranded on the beach for five uncomfortable days and five even more uncomfortable nights. In the meanwhile the men on the cutter had constructed a raft to which they attached two drums of water. Two more of the diamond hunters tried to reach the shore on the raft but were thrown off and only just managed to reach the beach with tremendous effort. At this point the police patrol, which had been on the look-out for them, arrived on the scene and instructed them to get back to the cutter, using the dinghy and when the sea was sufficiently calm. They were then to proceed to Walvis Bay and on arrival to report to the nearest police station. Broker had other ideas, however, and after retrieving the four men with the greatest of difficulty, set out for Mossamedes instead. Once there, he prepared for the return journey to Cape Town, but because of poor weather was forced to go ashore at Walvis Bay, where the diamond hunters were promptly arrested and Broker fined £40 for having landed them in a prohibited area. Although the experience put paid to any further attempts by these particular fortune hunters, they still insisted that there was a large diamond bonanza just waiting to be taken.

PIONEERING DAYS

The first prospector to acquire a mineral concession in the Skeleton Coast and Kaokoland from the authorities was well-known Namibian businessman Jack Levinson. His prospecting and mining grant covered the area between the Hoanib and the eighteenth latitude, extending to the interior past Opuwa into east Kaokoland. It was valid for the prospecting of all minerals, including salt and oil. Initially using his own capital, he assembled a prospecting outfit and started operations along the coast. After battling with the elements and the logistics of the operation for nearly a year he eventually found diamonds between the Hoanib and the Hoarusib Rivers. The diamonds were on average small, but of a high quality. Several other mining companies now also became interested, including Kimberley West and Rio Tinto, but the results were not sufficiently promising and they withdrew after a while.

In 1961 three brothers, Jasper, Koos and Fanie van der Westhuizen and a cousin, Jannie van der Westhuizen, farmers from the Keetmanshoop district, inspired by stories of diamond deposits on the Skeleton Coast, obtained a prospecting concession from the Administration of South West Africa to prospect for diamonds between the Ugab and the Uniab Rivers. They found diamonds at Toscanini, and also at a place further northwards, which they found visually so dreary that they defiantly named it Honolulu. They soon found that they were hopelessly undercapitalised and underequipped and proceeded to negotiate with several companies in order to obtain financial backing for their operation. At the same time they became interested in the concession area north of the Hoanib River up to the Kunene which then belonged to Jack Levinson, where they were convinced the ultimate bonanza was bound to be found. By this time a fair amount of prospecting had already been done in the northern section and the opinion was that the mineral potential in general, and the diamond potential in particular, was minimal, and that other than small sporadic pockets there were no deposits worth mining. The Van der Westhuizens, however, believed with unwavering optimism that this was not a true reflection of the actual potential, that there were in fact vast diamond deposits and that it was merely a question of thorough prospecting. They sold their concession between the Ugab and the Uniab Rivers to Dr Peter le Riche, and started negotiations with Jack Levinson to buy his mineral rights.

Not having sufficient funds themselves, they formed a consortium with a number of their relatives and other farmers in the Keetmanshoop district and raised enough money to buy the concession, for which a company called Westies Minerals (Pty) Ltd was formed. Convinced that sooner or later they were going to hit the jackpot, the company started working the terraces near the existing Levinson camp. It was a shoestring operation from the start, however, to the extent that they had to make do with derelict equipment that was standing around, using wooden bearings to repair the old rusted diamond jigs and initially managing without equipment as basic as a radio telephone. Their wives and children were with them, and were living under the most crude and primitive of conditions. In January 1963, which was a good rain year, it started pouring down torrentially in the interior. All rivers, including the Hoanib, came down in flood and the Van der Westhuizens were completely stranded, cut off from obtaining fresh supplies and from civilisation. They were forced to eat fish for days on end and became so desperate for the taste of meat that on one occasion they encircled a springbok and killed it by throwing stones at it: they had no firearms with them, because they were in a Bantu, Nature Conservation and Diamond Area.

By this time they were finding small quantities of diamonds, of good quality, but again not very large. These they disposed of through the De Beers Central Selling Organisation. The floodwaters had impressed on them how complete was their isolation, and with their first 'diamond' cheque they bought a one-channel radio. At this stage Ernst Karlowa and Jannie Peters-Hollenberg joined the company as shareholders. They were to assist the Van der Westhuizens in the search for better deposits. The company was still leading a hand-to-mouth existence, hoping that it would eventually gain sufficiently from the proceeds to expand and buy better equipment. Despite their many trials and tribulations, the Van der Westhuizens were becoming attached to the harsh barren wastes of the Skeleton Coast, so much so that Fanie van der Westhuizen, upon his return from a holiday in his native Keetmanshoop — a rather dry and barren part of Namibia — when asked how he had enjoyed his sojourn, replied that he found Keetmanshoop far too green!

At the end of a two-year period of prospecting, however, the going was getting too rough even for the intrepid Van der Westhuizens, and they more or less decided to call it a day. The company was experiencing severe financial difficulties and could find no reliable financial backers. The only people prepared to invest money were those whose sole interest was to 'make a fast buck' by disposing of the concession as soon as possible, or as one of them cynically phrased it, 'Why spoil a perfectly good mineral proposition by disproving it?' In the end Westies Minerals became part of the new company called the Sarusas Development Corporation, a consortium of which several large and financially strong companies such as SANLAM, the Industrial and Development Corporation, Volkskas and the General Mining and Finance Corporation were also shareholders.

In the meanwhile, further south, Dr Peter le Riche, who had given up his medical practice to pursue other interests, one of which was prospecting, and who had bought the Ugab-Uniab concession from the Van der Westhuizen brothers, continued where they had left off. He formed a new company, Desert Diamonds (Pty) Ltd of which Sammy Collins of 'diamonds from the sea' fame, the artist Vladimir Tretchikoff and Johan Dohms became shareholders. The latter had been lured back to the Skeleton Coast after a period of twenty years. He had been the navigator of the Ventura bomber which had come to grief in the course of the *Dunedin Star* rescue operation. In those days he had been told of the 'stones' of the Skeleton Coast and had always had a yearning to return. In the intervening years he had become an expert at erecting and managing prospecting

89

92

93

94

plants. He was given the task of erecting and operating the plant at Toscanini, as the new mine was to be called. After a few months, however, they began to lose confidence in the diamond potential. When they realised that the mine was not going to become viable and that they stood to lose their money, Collins, Dohms and Tretchikoff withdrew from the venture. Despite a period of extremely prosperous years on the Namibian diamond scene, Collins, a colourful and dynamic character, died a lonely pauper in London's East End a few years ago. Peter le Riche finally sold out lock, stock and barrel to Ben du Preez and his associate Colonel Jack Scott, a man of considerable wealth and at that stage still the largest private shareholder of the General Mining and Finance Corporation and of which he had in former years been the managing director.

THE AMETHYST MINE AT SARUSAS

Although Sarusas amethysts are considered to be of the best in the world as far as quality is concerned, mining them has never proved to be economically viable. During the 1950s and 1960s, when various individuals and concerns held concessions on the Skeleton Coast, it was known that amethyst occurred in the Etendeka lavas of the coastal areas and that the most obvious occurrence was among the lava hills about 16 km north-west of the Sarusas Fountain in the Khumib River course. In 1962 when Westies Minerals took over Jack Levinson's concession north of the Hoanib River, the amethyst geodes that contained the mauve and deep purple crystals could still be picked up from the surface. In 1963 the company was approached by a certain Erhard Gohlke, a goldsmith who had a

Opposite

92   A façade of fine river silt sandwiched between layers of coarser river mud adorns a bank of the Khumib River.

93   The vivid candelabra-like **Euphorbia virosa** has a milky latex which is poisonous. If it comes in contact with the eyes, it causes severe inflammation which could result in blindness.

94   The morning-glory-like flower of the sprawling vine **Merremia guerichii**, commonly called desert parsley because of the small, clustered leaves which resemble sprigs of parsley.

The remains of the oil drill erected by the intrepid Ben du Preez near the mouth of the Huab River.

jewellery business in Swakopmund. He and a friend, Lothar Schneider, were interested in mining the amethysts at Sarusas. Schneider was from Idar-Oberstein, the heart of the semi-precious stones industry in Germany, which, interestingly enough, owed its own development centuries ago to a similar kind of amethyst occurrence as the one at Sarusas. Westies Minerals entered into a partnership with Gohlke and Schneider, and a new company called Sarusas Minerals (Pty) Ltd was formed.

A camp was built in among a setting of bleak and wind-eroded lava hills and, having employed 15 labourers from Kaokoland and a white miner to run the operation, the mine went into production. The geodes were blasted out from the rock in which they were embedded and then, if they had not already broken open in the explosion, were forced open with heavy hammers to see whether the crystals inside were of suitable quality. The raw material was transported nearly 600 km to Walvis Bay and from there exported to Idar-Oberstein. Although the quality of the amethysts was high, the mine never became profitable. The logistics of transport and maintenance involved in an undertaking of this nature in such a remote area were always immense and there were continual problems with the control and management of the mine. Because the raw amethyst geodes were so bulky and costly to transport, the company decided that the crystals should be prepared for marketing at the mine by chopping away all the outer layers of agate and white quartz in order to export only the pure crystals. An expert was imported from Idar-Oberstein for this purpose, and was flown out from Germany and taken to Sarusas with the prospect of earning double his previous salary and numerous additional benefits. When two of the directors visited the mine a few days later they found him in a feverish state of hysteria and fear. He was finding it difficult to breathe, and refused point-blank to stay a day longer. He found the remoteness and loneliness of the area too much to bear and insisted on returning to Germany, which he did after little more than a week. In subsequent years the mine was worked from time to time, as renewed attempts were made to make it viable. Today it is abandoned, an ugly scar in an otherwise scenically beautiful section of the coast.

THE BIG-TIME PROSPECTORS

The Consolidated Diamond Mining Company, better known as C.D.M., also prospected on the Skeleton Coast. Having acquired, *inter alia*, a prospecting concession for the area between the Uniab and the Hoanib Rivers, operations were conducted from a base camp at Terrace Bay. Although diamonds were found, they were considered too small and the occurrences too sporadic to be mined economically and C.D.M. eventually gave up the concession voluntarily. It was taken up immediately by Ben du Preez and Colonel Jack Scott, who at that stage were active further south at Toscanini between the Ugab and Uniab Rivers where they were already operating a large and very expensive diamond-processing plant, rumoured at the time to have cost well over R2 million to erect. They apparently believed that even small diamonds could be lucrative if the dia-mondiferous gravels were handled in bulk quantities. Whatever the case may have been, without carrying out much further prospecting, they commenced opera-tions in the same concession area that C.D.M. had discarded after a thorough investigation and erected an even larger and more expensive plant at Terrace Bay. It was rumoured at the time that Du Preez, his wife and Colonel Scott held seances to divine the location of diamond and other deposits. The company had an unexpected windfall in terms of building material when the Portuguese vessel *Viente e Oito de Maio* ran aground just north of the Toscanini camp. She was carrying a large consignment of a good quality wood, which was promptly purchased and used for the further construction of the two mines.

For several years prospecting and mining were ostensibly carried out in the two adjoining areas, while the 'shy millionaire of the Skeleton Coast', as Du Preez had been dubbed by the media, gained in reputation as a romantic and somewhat mysterious figure. During this period he also erected a large tin-mining plant east of Cape Cross, which he called Strathmore Tin. He had become friendly with the Greek shipping magnate Aristotle Onassis and tried to interest him in taking up a share in the company. Onassis visited Terrace Bay with his son Alexander and, although he decided against investing in the company, he was sufficiently impressed by the area to exclaim, as he looked across the desert, 'What magnificent solitude!'

Despite being advised that it was highly unlikely that there was any oil to be found on the Skeleton Coast, they also bought and erected an oil drill at the Huab mouth. At the same time they built a bridge over the Huab River, the only one in the Skeleton Coast, and Du Preez named it after his partner. To this day the rather precarious-looking structure is known as the Jack Scott Bridge. Although they found no oil, they claimed that they had struck a rich anthracite deposit, but that on account of the depth did not at that stage consider exploiting it. In the late sixties Du Preez bought a spacious mansion in

The Jack Scott Bridge, seemingly quite solid from the air, is a narrow and precarious-looking structure which is very seldom used.

169

Houghton, Johannesburg. He had R80 000's worth of carpeting made to order, which depicted Skeleton Coast motifs such as welwitschia, gemsbok, ostrich and for the main reception room a diamond, as a gesture of recognition to the area that had been so 'good' to him. There was nothing small about the way in which Ben du Preez managed his affairs. The story is told of how in a particular instance he so liked the latest model of a luxury motor car that he ordered six. His company owned a luxury aircraft with which he regularly commuted between Johannesburg and Terrace Bay.

Then, inevitably, the company began to run into financial difficulties. The Standard Bank of South Africa had granted it an overdraft of more than R50 million to develop the mining potential of the area but, by the time the overdraft reached the R28 million mark, the bank realised that the affairs of the company were not healthy and stopped the facility. It was alleged *inter alia* that the company had a contract for the delivery of vast quantities of tin with a certain Hughes Aircraft Company, by implication connected with the mysterious American millionaire Howard Hughes. On closer examination, however, it transpired that the company in question was a small bogus concern which had no connection at all with Howard Hughes. When the bank finally decided to call it a day and refused to advance any more funds, Du Preez took the initiative and took it to court. Needless to say, the action eventually turned against him. When his company was finally liquidated the bank's claim amounted to R32 million, while the company's assets totalled hardly R1 million. The Department of Nature Conservation and Tourism bought the accommodation and store rooms at Terrace Bay and converted them into facilities for anglers, while the plant was sold as scrap.

This elaborate concrete bunker was built at Terrace Bay for storage of the diamonds that were never found.

History repeated itself when George Christodoulou appeared on the scene about ten years later. Backed by financial interests in the United States of America, he entered into a prospecting agreement with the Sarusas Development Corporation to prospect and mine for diamonds on the Skeleton Coast. He represented a certain George Osserman from the U.S.A., who in turn claimed that he represented various well-known American personalities, one of whom, according to the media, was Elvis Presley. He was to invest their money in different outlets in the world as part of a complicated tax-avoidance scheme.

Christodoulou initially operated from the old Sarusas mine, but soon realised that there were no diamonds to be had and, having churned up and disfigured much of the surroundings, moved his operations to Möwe Bay where the performance was repeated. He erected an impressive plant and a luxurious camp with recreational facilities which even included a swimming-pool — although it was never filled with water. Shortly after going into 'production', his company also ran into financial difficulties. It went into liquidation and Christodoulou promptly left the country. To judge by the newspaper reports, he lived well while the going was good. He owned two Rolls Royces, a Citation Executive Jet with which he commuted between Johannesburg, Windhoek and the Skeleton Coast, a helicopter, several piston-engined aeroplanes and an impressive fleet of motor vehicles. He posed as the Paraguayan consul to South Africa and to prove it, hung Paraguayan consular shields outside his house in Empire Place, Johannesburg, where he lived in opulence and style.

Whether George Christodoulou has been the last of the 'Big Spenders', at the expense of one of the world's few remaining wilderness areas, still remains to be seen. The current Director of Nature Conservation, Polla Swart, as did former Director Bernabé de la Bat, has initiated negotiations with the Department of Economic Affairs and Mining to discontinue the granting of mineral rights for prospecting in park areas. If these negotiations are successful, it could mean that the relentless disfigurement and pollution of the landscape will finally cease, although the defacement which has already taken place will, in human terms, be there forever.

Political History and Development

...the creation of a desert park

THE SKELETON COAST has had a chequered history in the sense that for almost eighty years the area has been protected on the one hand, but exploited on the other. Since 1907 access by the public has been restricted, for various considerations and different periods of time, in that it has been set aside as a Bantu Reserve, Nature Conservation Area and Diamond Area, for much of the time as all three concurrently. Prohibited area notwithstanding, the landscape has been subjected to varying degrees of defacement and pollution as a result of numerous prospecting and mining attempts, and the 'official' visits of countless bureaucrats for angling, hunting and holidaying purposes, while game numbers have steadily dwindled under the onslaught of poachers, with a particularly devastating effect on the vulnerable elephant and black rhino populations.

On 22 March 1907 the German Colonial Government proclaimed three game reserves, of which Game Reserve 2 comprised the Etosha National Park as it is known today and the entire Kaokoland from the Kunene River in the north to the Hoarusib River in the south, including the coastal section which later became known as the Skeleton Coast, a total surface area of 93 240 square kilometres. In 1923 three small Bantu Reserves were created in the Kaokoveld for Herero Headmen Oorlog, Katiti and Kasupi. In 1947 the entire Kaokoland section of Game Reserve 2 was declared as a Bantu Reserve 'for the sole use and occupation by natives', although at the time it was not deproclaimed as a game reserve. The area declared as a reserve extended as far south as the Hoanib River. In 1958, as recommended by the so-called 'Elephant Commission' of 1956, the unoccupied state land between the Hoanib and the Ugab Rivers was proclaimed part of Game Reserve 2, which by then was known as the Etosha National Park. It had become clear that the area was not big enough to accommodate rare and endangered species such as black rhino, mountain zebra and black-faced impala, migratory big game such as eland and elephant, and the influx of wildlife from adjacent areas. The extension of the boundaries to the west practically doubled the size of the park, which, extending from the Skeleton Coast in the west for nearly 500 km inland to the Etosha Pan in the east, covered a surface area of 99 526 square kilometres.

Unfortunately, the existence of what was effectively the largest national game reserve in the world was short-lived. As a result of the recommendations of the Odendaal Report of 1963, aimed at applying the South African policies of separate homeland development or 'apartheid' in Namibia and lessening her autonomy by managing her as a fifth province of South Africa, the park area was drastically reduced with a total disregard for ecological boundaries. 71 972 square kilometres were sacrificed to the land needs of the newly created homelands of Owambo, Kaokoland and Damaraland. The entire Kaokoland was deproclaimed as a game reserve, with the exception of the 30 to 40 km wide strip of coastline between the Kunene and the Ugab Rivers which, as a somewhat conciliatory gesture, was set aside to be developed as a tourist area.

Neither the Etosha National Park, which had been reduced in surface area

The goats of the Ovahimba present a threat to the wild animals, as they destroy the already sparse grazing of the marginal desert areas.

by 77 per cent, causing a furore of national and international proportions, nor the narrow strip of coastline which was subsequently proclaimed as the Skeleton Coast Park in 1971, made any kind of ecological sense. A large section of western Kaokoland and western Damaraland is totally unfit for agricultural development or human habitation. From an ecological point of view, it links up naturally with the Skeleton Coast Park. This section has been turned into a virtual wasteland because poachers have been able to go about their business of extermination unhindered. Once the animals, whose subsistence is the east/west river courses with their waterholes and riverine vegetation, move beyond the confines of the Skeleton Coast Park into the adjacent Kaokoland and Damaraland, they are in danger of falling prey to poachers and trophy hunters. The shrinkage of the Etosha National Park cut off natural migration patterns and it soon became necessary to cull large numbers of animals on an annual basis, in order to conserve grazing and prevent game from moving to adjacent farms.

Another result of the implementation of the Odendaal proposals was that the migratory elephant population became divided into two geographically separated groups. The increase in human activity in the homelands forced a section of the game westwards, separating it from the main populations in the east. A large number of elephant stopped migrating out of Etosha altogether, while part of the western population took up occupation of the west-flowing river courses in Damaraland and Kaokoland and became the much-publicised 'desert' elephants, giving rise to the myth that they were a separate species with special adaptations which distinguished them from the elephants of Etosha. These elephants were constantly exposed to poaching and trophy hunting for they inhabited an area where there was little control, to the extent that the survival of this particular population has now become endangered. In Etosha, on the other hand, the growing numbers of elephant have become increasingly problematical, necessitating culling on an annual basis — a practice which is both unpopular and entails operational complications of a considerable magnitude, such as erecting an abattoir in the bush and transporting the meat in special cool trucks for 500 km to the processing factory at Oshakati. A solution would be to extend the boundaries of the Skeleton Coast Park as far east into Damaraland and Kaokoland as possible and to create a corridor linking up with the Etosha National Park, thereby reinstating natural migration routes and preserving what is scenically one of the most beautiful, and ecologically one of the most unusual, desert environments in the world. The enlarged park could, if managed correctly, be of substantial political and economic significance to Namibia in the future.

ATTEMPTED DEVELOPMENT OF AN INFRASTRUCTURE

During the sixties the idea of building a harbour north of Swakopmund was once again considered. At this stage the Skeleton Coast was a prohibited area on three counts. To so much as enter three separate permits needed to be obtained, from three different State departments, namely, those of Bantu Affairs, Nature Conservation and Mines. Since 1962 the company Westies Minerals, which held the concession rights for the area between the Hoanib River and the eighteenth latitude, had been mining diamonds on a small scale at Möwe Bay, and was also doing a certain amount of prospecting further afield. After a period of two years, undercapitalisation and the high cost of mining in such a remote area forced the company to cease operations.

95

96

97

During this time the directors of Westies Minerals had become increasingly aware of the vast potential of the rich fishing grounds adjoining their concession area. The idea was born that exploitation of these resources could be applied to support a more substantial prospecting programme, both for minerals along the coast as well as in the hinterland. The creation of an infrastructure, including a harbour, an airfield and a road to the north, while supporting the proposed fishing industry, would in itself be a major contribution towards reducing the prohibitively high prospecting costs, and would at the same time promote development in other spheres. The fishing industry would be the growth point around which secondary industries, such as the production of salt and processing of cattle meat from Owambo and Kaokoland, could develop.

Up to this point the government had not required any compensation for the fishing concessions that they granted for exploiting resources off the Namibian coast. This unhealthy state of affairs was further aggravated by the fact that the concessions were handed out indiscriminately with little regard to possible overutilisation of resources. The directors of Westies Minerals put forward the proposal that in exchange for fishing rights along the Skeleton Coast, the company would build a harbour, airfield and road to the north, which would

Opposite
96 Acting as a lens rather than a mirror, the atmosphere produces images by refraction, which advance and recede as the viewer moves backwards and forwards.

97 'Skull Rock', situated in the lower reaches of the Munutum River, acts as a stark reminder of many a mariner who came to grief on the Skeleton Coast.

The old observation post at Angra Fria used by Ernst Karlowa during the hydrographical research programme.

become government property on completion. To further these proposals a new consortium was formed. It consisted of the old Westies Company and several large and more illustrious companies such as SANLAM, Volkskas, General Mining and the Industrial Development Corporation. Well-known personalities such as Dr A. D. Wassenaar, Dr Tommie Muller, Dr van Eck and Dr Hurter, at the time chairmen respectively of SANLAM, General Mining, I.D.C. and Volkskas, were involved, and the new company was called the Sarusas Development Corporation. It took over the existing mineral concession and entered into an agreement with the Administration of South West Africa regarding the implementation of the development proposals and undertook to encourage other large companies to invest in the development of the area. The then Administrator of the Territory, Wennie du Plessis, was very much in favour of the scheme and gave the consortium the full support of the South West African Government.

One of the first decisions to make was where to build the harbour. Ernst Karlowa was appointed to erect a research station at Angra Fria, a site which had been chosen because it was accessible from the interior, had a reasonable bay and because the adjacent salt-pans could be tested for their suitability as regards a possible salt industry. When Karlowa left Swakopmund with two 15-ton Leyland trucks and a Chevrolet lorry loaded with the materials needed to build the station, he was regarded with considerable scepticism. It was thought unlikely that he would be able to travel through the dune area with such heavy vehicles. After four gruelling days, however, using tarred poles as temporary 'railroads' he managed to reach Angra Fria. The camp was erected partially from the material brought from Swakopmund, and partially from wood from wreckage collected on the beach.

The Council for Scientific and Industrial Research, which headed the harbour research programme, came to the conclusion after two years that the site was unsuitable. The camp was moved 200 km south to Möwe Bay, where a similar research programme was carried out, this time with the assistance of Christiani & Nielsen, an international engineering firm which specialised in building harbours. During this period, thanks to the endeavours of Peter le Riche, Ben du Preez and Jack Scott as well as the new company, the road from the Ugab River to the north was gradually extended until it finally reached Möwe Bay in 1968. This is still the northernmost point to which an ordinary vehicle can travel. In the same year a provisional airfield was built at Möwe Bay, and the harbour research programme was completed. Möwe Bay had been found suitable for the purpose of building a harbour. The initial design made provision for accommodating a cargo ship with a capacity of up to 15 000 tons and several fishing vessels, while allowing for possible future extensions.

In the meantime, as a result of the implementation of the Odendaal proposals and to tighten the link between South West Africa and South Africa, important state departments such as Economic Affairs and Sea Fisheries were taken over by the South African Government. It became clear from the outset that the latter was opposed to the idea of building a harbour. When the Sarusas Development Corporation was finally preparing to call for tenders to build the harbour at Möwe Bay, the directors were summoned to Cape Town and summarily informed that the government did not wish them to proceed with their plans and was withdrawing unilaterally from the contract. The reasons given were that fishing activities on the northern section of the coast could be detrimental to the Walvis Bay and Lüderitz industries. The result was that the entire development project was scrapped.

By this time, due to overfishing, resources off the Namibian coast, particularly in the south, were already seriously in jeopardy. In 1968 the Namibian and South African fleets had landed a record 1,5 million tons of fish. Dr Jan Lochner, former head of the Port Elizabeth Oceanographic Institute, warned that without proper control the resources, unlimited as they seemed, would soon be depleted. His warnings were largely ignored. Apart from the South African factory ships, large numbers of foreign ships were fishing off the coast, ignoring the local closed seasons, fishing boundaries and international regulations. Not long after this came the dramatic collapse of the Namibian fishing industry. It is interesting, however, that to this day fishing off the Skeleton Coast portion of the Namibian coastline is still good and that most of the fish at present being processed by the factories in Walvis Bay is hauled over long distances and at great expense from those waters.

The boards which demarcate the eastern border of the 25-40 km narrow park. This border should be moved much further inland to make the park ecologically viable.

Following the South African government's withdrawal from the agreement, the Sarusas Development Corporation donated the buildings, vehicles and equipment at Möwe Bay, and a sum of R25 000, to the Department of Nature Conservation and Tourism on condition that it be applied to promote conservation and tourism in the area. The then Director of the Department, Bernabé de la Bat, was able to use this offer as a lever to expedite the necessary legislation to give effect to the recommendations of the Odendaal Plan, and the Skeleton Coast Park was finally proclaimed in 1971.

Tourism and Conservation

... preservation of a wilderness area

IN A RECENT lecture entitled 'Tourism and Conservation: Can they coexist in arid environments?', ecologist Professor Clifford S. Crawford of the University of New Mexico, Albuquerque, U.S.A. argued that '... unless tourism in dry climates is kept within the bounds of ecological tolerance, the future of the industry, as well as the resource it exploits, will soon be irreversibly damaged'. Tourism in an arid region is potentially self-limiting in that large numbers of visitors represent a serious threat to its easily disrupted ecosystem. Access by visitors should therefore be monitored in accordance with the 'carrying capacity' of the area. Disturbing the ecological balance and the inevitable defacement that goes hand in hand with an infrastructure developed to cater for heavy tourist traffic would soon destroy the very thing that people set out to enjoy.

Because it is the more discerning tourist who appreciates what a desert area has to offer and leaves what he sees behind as he found it, the approach to tourism in the Skeleton Coast Park has been from the outset to cater for quality tourism as opposed to quantity tourism. Since its inception in 1971 it has been managed as a wilderness reserve, where wilderness is defined as 'an area where the earth and its community of life are untrammelled by man, where man himself is a visitor who does not remain'. Today the need for wilderness reserves is universally recognised. It vests in their aesthetic value as landscapes unscarred by roads,

Wandering barchan dunes only temporarily cover the unsightly vehicle tracks.

railway lines or power lines, the opportunities they offer in physical and spiritual recreation, their scientific interest as natural ecosystems and, albeit a somewhat nebulous concept, the mere knowledge that they are there. In the frenetic world of today there is a growing awareness of the equilibrium and perspective that wilderness areas generate in the minds of those who visit them.

The result has been a pronounced upswing in the numbers of tourists visiting the wilderness areas of the world, especially from European countries, which in many cases has led to overutilisation of the area, more often than not to the extent that the damage is irrevocable. Consequently, the obvious attraction and less obvious ecological integrity of many of these areas are fast diminishing. Overexposure of a fragile ecological system such as the Namib Desert will inevitably have its detrimental effects. Not only is it a closed ecological circuit, but the tempo is slow, recovery takes long and the balance is extremely delicate. The highly specialised fauna cannot exist beyond the dunes. Exposure to tourism should therefore be allowed only after careful consideration of the intrinsic nature of the area in question.

On the one hand the Skeleton Coast has been favourably positioned from the outset to be effectively protected as a wilderness reserve. Namibia is a vast country with a sparse population which is largely rural, and consequently internal pressure on her desert areas has been rather less than in, for instance, the U.S.A., where the population of 250 million is largely urban and the need for 'getting away from it all' is far more actual and pressing. From as far back as 1907 access to the Skeleton Coast has, for political and various other considerations, been restricted and the area therefore closed to the general public. The mere fact of its geographical isolation has further protected it. On the other hand, lured by legendary stories of lost treasure and hidden mineral wealth, even its remotest

corners are to this day subjected to defacement by prospectors, miners, explorers and treasure hunters, not to mention poachers, who will relentlessly hunt down the last remnants of the dwindling animal populations.

The only way to combine conservation and tourism in this kind of environment is to keep development to a minimum and to restrict the numbers of visiting tourists. The attraction of the Skeleton Coast lies essentially in the vastness, changing moods and untouched profile of its landscape. These qualities can be retained only by reducing as far as possible the impact of visitors. Promotion should be directed towards the kind of people who are interested in the specific qualities of the area, the opinion-makers who will take the concept of conservation away with them. Generally, the tourists from Europe prefer facilities and accommodation that are simple but effective. They come to see the country in its natural state and to experience the silence, solitude and mystique of the desert environment. They wish to get away from the foyers of luxury hotels and large 'marina'-type developments, and most of all from other people.

These principles have largely been followed by the Directorate of Nature Conservation in its management of the Skeleton Coast Park. In the southern section tourism is restricted to two angling resorts, with access along a coastal route or from the interior. Torra Bay, a camping site, and Terrace Bay, a small self-contained rest-camp, have boundaries within which visitors must remain. Visitors to the northern section of the park are restricted to fly-in safaris and are limited to a maximum of twelve visitors at a time. Accommodation is in tents at a base camp with basic facilities and visitors are taken around in the area by four-wheel drive under the supervision of an expert guide along different routes to such features as the roaring dunes near Rocky Point, the white castles of the

The specialist knowledge of the television cameraman ensures a visual access to wilderness reserves that is often superior to that which would normally be gained by being on the spot.

The camping site at Torra Bay caters for angling enthusiasts.

Hoarusib Canyon, the seals of Cape Frio and the Agate Mountain.

Long hiking trips are not practicable in the park proper because of lack of water. Supervised hikes are, however, conducted by Nature Conservation officials along the Ugab River course, the southern border of the park. An aspect which is often overlooked is the fact that, because of the remoteness and isolation of the area, there is considerable risk involved when travelling without a guide or thorough knowledge of the terrain, which can — and it has on occasion — lead to disaster. A guide is especially necessary to point out the many different points and places of interest, which would otherwise be missed. In addition, people not acquainted with the area who drive around looking for specific features inevitably make new and unnecessary tracks, at present one of the most prevalent forms of pollution in the park.

In a world that is shrinking at an explosive rate the inevitable question arises: Can the setting aside of wilderness reserves to which entrance is restricted to an 'elitist' few be reasonably justified? The answer is that this is the only way that such areas can survive. By way of artists, photographers and film-makers the wilderness idea can be conveyed to those who are unable to visit such reserves themselves. The specialist knowledge of the cameraman will bring to people all over the world, whether in the centre of London or Berlin, in New York or Tokyo, a visual access to wilderness and desert reserves which is in many ways superior to that gained by being there in person.

Desert reserves such as the Skeleton Coast Park are valuable assets which in a hundred years might well have more intrinsic worth to mankind than oil or uranium, and as such they should be protected beyond the boundaries of ideology and politics, regardless of the countries in which they are situated and the government of the day. It is ironic that those countries which still have wilderness areas to protect often lack both the funds and the inclination to do so, whereas countries which have the funds and the needs have long since sacrificed such areas to civilisation. In a sense the remaining wilderness areas belong to all mankind. The obligation to protect them lies not only in the country where they are located but also with those countries which make use of them or are likely to do so in the future.

Bibliography

Andersson, C.J., *Explorations and Discoveries in South-Western Africa*, facsimile reprint (Cape Town, 1967).

Bannister, Anthony and Johnson, Peter, *Namibia, Africa's Harsh Paradise*, 1st ed. (Cape Town, 1978).

Berry, H.H., 'Cormorants' lives are dominated by the wind', *S.W.A. Annual 1980* (Windhoek, 1980).

Brittan, Michael, *Discover Namibia*, 1st ed. (Cape Town, 1979).

Buys, P.J. and P.J.C., *Slange van Suidwes-Afrika* (Windhoek, 1984).

Clement, A.J., 'Ogden's Harbour — a South West mystery', *S.W.A. Annual 1983* (Windhoek, 1983).

Clinning, Charles, 'Birds of the Namib', *S.W.A. Annual 1981* (Windhoek, 1981).

Cooke, Ronald U. and Warren, Andrew, *Geomorphology in Deserts*, 1st ed. (London, 1975).

Court, Doreen, *Succulent Flora of Southern Africa*, 1st ed. (Cape Town, 1981).

Crawford, Clifford S., 'Tourism and Conservation: Can they coexist in arid environments?', lecture (Windhoek, 1983).

Cubitt, Gerald and Richter, Johann, *South West*, 1st ed. (Cape Town, 1976).

Davis, Nissen, 'They motored up the Skeleton Coast', *S.W.A. Annual 1956* (Windhoek, 1956).

Davis, Sam, 'Ashore Cape Frio', *S.W.A. Annual 1946* (Windhoek, 1946).
    'How Skeleton Coast was named', *S.W.A. Annual 1978* (Windhoek, 1978).
    'Shipwreck dramas of the Coast of S.W.A.', *S.W.A. Annual 1946* (Windhoek, 1946).
    'Salvage on Skeleton Coast', *S.W.A. Annual 1968* (Windhoek, 1968).
    'Skeleton Coast — 1966 *Viente E. Oito de Maio*' *S.W.A. Annual 1967* (Windhoek, 1967).
    'Torpedoed off the Skeleton Coast', *S.W.A. Annual 1952* (Windhoek, 1952).
    'The voyage of the *Theodora*', *S.W.A. Annual 1947* (Windhoek, 1947).

De le Bat, B.J.G., 'Etosha 75 Years', *S.W.A. Annual 1982* (Windhoek, 1982).

Dorst, Jean and Dandelot, Pierre, *A Field Guide to the Larger Mammals of Africa*, 2nd ed. (London, 1980).

Fraser, Alistair B. and Mach, William H., 'Mirages', *Scientific American* (U.S.A., 1976).

Green, Lawrence G., *Lords of the Last Frontier*, 1st ed. (Cape Town, 1952).

Hartmann, Georg, 'Meine Expedition 1900 ins nördliche Kaokoland und 1901 durch des Amboland', paper (Dresden, Germany, 1902).
    Two letters to Major T.H. Leutwein (Swakopmund and Walvis Bay, 1886).

Joubert, Eugéne, 'Die Swart Renoster', *S.W.A. Annual 1983* (Windhoek, 1983).

Koch, Charles, 'Living Sands', *S.W.A. Annual 1970* (Windhoek, 1970).

Kutscher, C.F., *Geschrieben unter dem Kameldornbaum,* 1st ed. (Windhoek, 1982).

   Wanderungen und Kämpfe in Südwestafrika, Ostafrika und Südafrika, 1st ed. (Windhoek, 1982).

Logan, Richard F., 'The strangest Climate', *S.W.A. Annual 1970* (Windhoek, 1970).

Marsh, John H., *Skeleton Coast,* 1st ed. (London, 1944).

Müller, M.A.N., *Grasse van Suidwes-Afrika/Namibië,* 1st ed. (Windhoek, 1982).

Nieman, W.A., Heyns, C. and Seely, M.K., 'A note on precipitation at Swakopmund', *Madoqua* Vol. 11, No. 1 (Windhoek, 1978).

Newman, Kenneth, *Newman's Birds of Southern Africa,* 1st ed. (Johannesburg, 1983).

Palgrave, Keith Coates, *Trees of Southern Africa,* 1st ed. (Cape Town, 1977).

Palmer, Eve, *Trees of Southern Africa,* 1st ed. (Cape Town, 1972).

Penrith, Mary-Louise, 'The species of *Onymacris* Allard (Coleoptera: Tenebrionidae)', *Cimbebasia,* Ser. A, Vol. 4, No. 3 (Windhoek, 1975).

Roberts, Austin, *Roberts' Birds of South Africa,* revised ed., by McLachlan and Liversidge (Cape Town, 1982).

Schoeman, Amy, 'The Lure of the Skeleton Coast', *S.W.A. Annual 1978* (Windhoek, 1978).

   ''n Kwarteeu Natuurbewaring en Toerisme', S.W.A. Annual 1980 (Windhoek, 1980).

   'Dunes of the Namib', *S.W.A. Annual 1981* (Windhoek 1981).

   'Taking a New Look at the Oldest Desert in the World', *S.W.A. Annual 1981* (Windhoek, 1981).

   'Wilderness and its Preservation in South West Africa', *S.W.A. Annual 1982* (Windhoek, 1982).

   'The lesser-known rivers of the north', *S.W.A. Annual 1983* (Windhoek, 1983).

   Notes on Nature, 1st ed. (Windhoek, 1984).

Seely, M.K., 'Fog Consumers of the Namib Desert', *S.W.A. Annual 1978* (Windhoek, 1978).

Selby, M.J., 'On the origin of sheeting and laminae in granitic rocks: evidence from Antarctica, the Namib Desert and the Central Sahara', *Madoqua,* Vol. 10, No. 3 (Windhoek, 1977).

Shaughnessy, P.D., 'Cape Fur Seals in South West Africa', *S.W.A. Annual 1979* (Windhoek, 1979).

Shortridge, G.C., *The Mammals of South West Africa,* Vols 1 & 2, 1st eds. (London, 1934).

Steyn, Herman, 'The Namib', *S.W.A. Annual 1978* (Windhoek, 1978).

Vedder, H., *Die Voorgeskiedenis van Suidwes-Afrika,* 1st ed. (Windhoek, 1937).

Van der Riet, Willem and Rowe, Gordon, 'Exploring the Cunene in Canoes', *S.W.A. Annual 1967* (Windhoek, 1967).

Von Schumann, Gunter, E., 'Lost Treasures of the Skeleton Coast', *Rössing,* September 1982 (Windhoek, 1982).

Ward, J.D., Seely, M.K. and Lancaster, N., 'On the Antiquity of the Namib', *South African Journal of Science,* Vol. 79, 175-83 (Johannesburg, 1983).

INDEX

Numbers in **bold** denote pages on which illustrations occur.